MAGICAL ASTROLOGY
FOR WITCHES

A Beginner Witch's Guide to Working Magic with the Planets and the Zodiac, with Spells, Oil Blends, and Divination Spreads

LISA CHAMBERLAIN & KIKI DOMBROWSKI

Magical Astrology for Witches

Copyright © 2023 by Lisa Chamberlain.

All rights reserved. No part of this book may be reproduced in any form without permission in writing from the author. Reviewers may quote brief passages in reviews

Published by **Chamberlain Publications (Wicca Shorts)**

ISBN-13: 978-1-912715-33-6

Disclaimer

No part of this publication may be reproduced or transmitted in any form or by any means, mechanical or electronic, including photocopying or recording, or by any information storage and retrieval system, or transmitted by email without permission in writing from the publisher.

While all attempts have been made to verify the information provided in this publication, neither the author nor the publisher assumes any responsibility for errors, omissions, or contrary interpretations of the subject matter herein.

This book is for entertainment purposes only. The views expressed are those of the author alone, and should not be taken as expert instruction or commands. The reader is responsible for his or her own actions.

Adherence to all applicable laws and regulations, including international, federal, state, and local governing professional licensing, business practices, advertising, and all other aspects of doing business in the US, Canada, or any other jurisdiction is the sole responsibility of the purchaser or reader.

Neither the author nor the publisher assumes any responsibility or liability whatsoever on the behalf of the purchaser or reader of these materials.

Any perceived slight of any individual or organization is purely unintentional.

YOUR FREE GIFT

Thank you for adding this book to your Wiccan library! To learn more, why not join Lisa's Wiccan community and get an exclusive, free spell book?

The book is a great starting point for anyone looking to try their hand at practicing magic. The ten beginner-friendly spells can help you to create a positive atmosphere within your home, protect yourself from negativity, and attract love, health, and prosperity.

Little Book of Spells is now available to read on your laptop, phone, tablet, Kindle or Nook device.

To download, simply visit the following link:

www.wiccaliving.com/bonus

GET THREE FREE AUDIOBOOKS FROM LISA CHAMBERLAIN

Did you know that all of Lisa's books are available in audiobook format? Best of all, you can get **three audiobooks completely free** as part of a 30-day trial with Audible.

Wicca Starter Kit contains three of Lisa's most popular books for beginning Wiccans, all in one convenient place. It's the best and easiest way to learn more about Wicca while also taking audiobooks for a spin! Simply visit:

www.wiccaliving.com/free-wiccan-audiobooks

Alternatively, *Spellbook Starter Kit* is the ideal option for building your magical repertoire using candle and color magic, crystals and mineral stones, and magical herbs. Three spellbooks —over 150 spells—are available in one free volume, here:

www.wiccaliving.com/free-spell-audiobooks

Audible members receive free audiobooks every month, as well as exclusive discounts. It's a great way to experiment and see if audiobook learning works for you.

If you're not satisfied, you can cancel anytime within the trial period. You won't be charged, and you can still keep your books!

CONTENTS

Preface 10

Introduction 13

    How to Get the Most out of This Book 15
    A Brief History of Astrology.. 17
    Basics in Astrology 19
        The Zodiac... 19
        The Elements... 20
        Modalities.. 20
        Planets and Celestial Bodies.. 21
        Your Natal Chart... 22
    Connecting with the Heavens (A Meditation) 25

Chapter One: **The Elements**... 28

    The Element of Fire... 30
    The Element of Earth 36
    The Element of Air 42
    The Element of Water... 48
    Elemental Card Spread... 55
    Experiencing the Elements in Your Body
    (A Meditation)... 57

Chapter Two: **Planet Power** 59

    The Sun 62
    The Moon 66

Mercury 70
Venus 73
Mars 77
Jupiter 80
Saturn 84
Uranus 87
Neptune 91
Pluto 94
Other Celestial Bodies 97
Planetary Divination Spread 100

Chapter Three: Our Enchanted Zodiac 102

The Big Three 104
Aries 108
Taurus 112
Gemini 115
Cancer 119
Leo 122
Virgo 125
Libra 129
Scorpio 132
Sagittarius 136
Capricorn 140
Aquarius 144
Pisces 148
Zodiac Sign Reflections 151

Chapter Four: The Mystical Moon 153

Lunar Phases 154
The Moon's Movement Through the Zodiac Signs 160
Void Moon *166*

Special Moons 167
Full Moon Waters 169
Lunar Calendar Journaling Exercise 170
Lunar Phase Divination Spread 171

Chapter Five: Our Magical Skies 174

Solar and Lunar Eclipses 175
Planets in Retrograde 177
Mercury in Retrograde Altar Set Up 182
Comets and Meteor Showers in Astrology 184
Meteor Show Magic through the Year 186
Wish Upon a Star Bay Leaf Spell 189

Conclusion 191

Suggestions for Further Reading 194
About the Authors 196

PREFACE

I'll never forget the first time I had an astrology reading. It was with a self-described shamanic astrologer, in a delightful little metaphysical bookstore in the upper Midwest. When I walked out of that hour-long conversation, I had a new understanding of how my Sun sign (Scorpio), Rising sign (Aquarius) and Moon sign (Leo) have shaped my experiences, perceptions, and responses to life.

I learned some new details as well. Most significantly, I have Venus and Mars in Scorpio, along with the Sun. Three or more planets in one sign is known as a "stellium," and this indicates that a person's life will be more dominated by that sign than any others. Given that it's considered intense enough to have one of the inner planets in Scorpio, let alone three, I'm not surprised that I get a few wary looks when I tell people about my chart!

Of course, Scorpio is considered to be one of the witchiest signs of the zodiac, as it governs occult knowledge and the psychic realms, so this stellium makes perfect sense to me. But the truth is that every sign has its own unique magical gifts—and you don't even have to be a witch to benefit from them.

Astrology can help everyone, regardless of magical inclinations, in two major ways. First, it offers an understanding of how the movements of the planets affect the events unfolding here on Earth, both in our collective reality and in our personal lives. Second, and perhaps more importantly, it helps us understand ourselves on a deeper level, through the signs that most significantly shape the way we experience life, and how we relate to others.

Witches (who fall under every sign, by the way) have the added advantage of being able to work actively with these two currents of understanding. For example, knowing the energetic cosmic patterns of a given period in time can helps us choose the most effective goals to work for at that moment. Furthermore, understanding how the celestial snapshot at the moment of our birth has shaped us as individuals can help us discover our personal best approaches to magic.

Kiki Dombrowski, my co-author, has her own unique take on astrological magic, and it was a delight to work with her on this collaboration. Kiki is a well-known writer on all things magical, as well as a teacher and life coach. This book grew out of her vision, and the bulk of the content is her own. I have edited the initial draft and added significant detail to several of the chapters. I hope you will find these pages as illuminating as I have, and be inspired to explore the relationship between magic and astrology even further.

Taken as a whole, the discipline of astrology shows us the divine intelligence of the universe. Whether you're brand new to astrology or have been studying it for years, this book will help you make the most of this divine wisdom—not only with the magic you practice, but also in your spiritual self-growth throughout this lifetime. Here's wishing you a rich and rewarding journey through the magic of the cosmos.

— Lisa Chamberlain, Editor and Co-author

INTRODUCTION: THE HEAVENS AS THE REALM OF THE GODS, PREDICTION, AND MAGIC

Humans have always been enchanted by the stars and aware of their influence in our lives. The heavens were the realm of the Gods, where the planets and stars were seen to move in patterns that impacted life here on Earth. Naturally, through a combination of precise observations, calculations, charting, and a worship of nature, the field of astrology blossomed.

Astrology is a complex and in-depth system of charting the celestial bodies' movements through the sky. The location of certain celestial bodies—within the sky itself and with relationship to each other— can influence a person on a deeply personal level. These movements can also influence worldly events.

Astrology is a lifetime study. Students of astrology may research many different topics within astrology for years before they feel they've mastered it. While it can be a complex field of study and practice, this should not put us off from exploring it and using astrology, even if we do not intend on reaching a level of mastery. Even understanding some of the basics can support us in our magic and enrich our understandings of ourselves and those in our lives.

In his book *Astrology for Witches*, Michael Herkes points out that "the more a witch understands astrological forces, the more they will be able to connect the dots to other aspects of the craft." The magical world weaves into the tapestry of the astrological sky. Witches, Wiccans, Pagans, and other members of the magical community have long known the benefits of utilizing astrology in their practice.

Plants, oils, and crystals have been assigned astrological correspondences that can help us choose the most beneficial ingredients for our spells and magical concoctions, to draw in the specific energy we're intending for. Certain days, astrological phases, and even seasons can help determine the best time to perform rituals, cast spells, or make influential life decisions.

Understanding astrology can also allow for us to deepen our understanding of divination—using horoscopes to create predictions, or even utilizing astrological correspondences in tarot, palmistry, or other divination tools. Most importantly, astrology gives you the opportunity to deepen your understanding of who you are and how you interact and respond with the heavens, allowing you to access and enhance your astrological magic.

HOW TO GET
THE MOST
OUT OF THIS BOOK

This book is meant to be a magical guide for witches who are curious about understanding the basics of astrology. It is meant to support you in your exploration of astrology and show you how it can be beneficial to your magical work, as well as deepening your spiritual sense of self. To get the most out of the information in this book, I recommend taking the following steps:

- **Print out your Natal Chart.** First, in preparation for this book, please consider printing out your natal chart, which is a chart of the sky at the exact moment you are born. This will allow you to reflect on your own chart and the celestial influences in your life as you progress through the chapters. An easy place to find your personal astrological data is at **www.astro.com**. Simply plug in the date, time, and location of your birth. You may also enjoy the popular phone app Co-Star, where you can read daily horoscopes and learn about your personal natal chart as well.

    To get the maximum benefit from your chart, you'll need to know your time of birth, which provides your Rising sign, as well as other details key to in-depth astrological readings. Try to find your birth time if you don't know it, but don't worry if you can't—you can still get plenty of useful insight in a chart using your date and place of birth.

- **Keep your "Big Three" in mind.** Your "Big Three" refers to three significant placements within your natal chart. These three placements can reveal a lot about your personality based on the zodiac, as well as how the stars influence your life. The "Big Three" include your Sun sign, Moon sign, and Rising sign. We will discuss these three signs in greater detail further along in this introduction, as well as in Chapter 3.

- **Keep a journal.** You may find that a special journal for your explorations is an excellent place to record your discoveries about yourself, your astrological research, and your magical work as it applies to astrology. There are also plenty of astrological planners and almanacs with room for writing and journaling throughout the year, such as the *Magic of I* journal. You may even enjoy the *Old Farmer's Almanac*, which has a lot of agricultural and astrological folklore within its pages. A journal allows you to learn by reflecting on your discoveries and experiences—for example, how that love spell you cast during a new moon on a Friday unfolded, or how you felt during a solar eclipse, or what steps you took to have a smooth Mercury retrograde.

- **Review the Recommended Reading at the end of the book.** Consider this book a useful tool for introducing you to astrology and how it can blend into your magical work. If you are looking to go deeper, the books recommended at the end of the book will assist you with furthering your study.

A BRIEF HISTORY OF ASTROLOGY

Astrology has been with us since the dawn of civilization, with our most ancient of ancestors looking to the heavens for support in daily life decisions, such as when to sow seeds or harvest crops. Cultures around the world have always been observing the stars, charting their movement and location with wonder and honor. And while this brief overview presents a linear timeline of developments in astrology; in reality, the cross-pollination of different cultures within the ancient world would have been more simultaneous and complex than the scope of this discussion allows.

When we think about the invention of modern astrology, we celebrate the ingenuity of the Mesopotamian cultures. Sumerians worshiped the sun, moon and Venus and discovered Mercury, Mars, Jupiter, and Saturn. They intuited the traits and properties of each planet and assigned an animal to each season: the bull was assigned to spring (Taurus), the lamb was assigned to summer, the scorpion was assigned to autumn (Scorpio), and the turtle was assigned to winter.

The Babylonians brought deeper development to astrology, dividing the sky into 12 equal parts and creating zodiac signs within these divisions. While the zodiac was originally used for grand predictions that involved agriculture, weather, and politics, in the 5th century BCE Babylonian astrology evolved into a more personalized examination of human traits and predictions. After Babylonia was conquered by Alexander the Great in 331 BCE, astrology was assimilated into Greek, and then Roman culture.

Astrology was not exclusive to these ancestors of "Western" culture, however. The ancient Hindus, for example, believed the god Vishnu took form of a ram, bull, or lion when he visited earth. According to Marion D. March and Joan McEvers in *The Only Way to Learn Astrology*, this is the foundation where we developed the signs Aries, Taurus, and Leo.

The Egyptians also had a deep and profound connection to the stars, building many temples and sacred places in alignment with significant constellations. The Chinese developed their own unique astrological system, developing a zodiac which follows the moon, rather than the constellations, and runs in 12-year cycles, rather than 12-month cycles. Each year of the cycle is symbolized by an animal, which is associated with the personality traits of everyone born in that year.

The astrology we work with today is based on the scholarship and magic of all these ancient cultures. However, modern day discoveries of celestial bodies such as Uranus, Neptune, Pluto, and various dwarf planets and asteroids have been incorporated into today's astrology to create an even more complex and rich study. The beauty of astrology is that as we discover more about the heavens, astrology evolves and expands.

BASICS IN ASTROLOGY

Let us briefly look at the foundational elements of astrology before moving forward into a more detailed study. There are many moving parts and complex layers to astrology, but here we will outline the basics that will help you to incorporate astrology into your magical practices. While some of these topics will be covered in detail within the book, others are more advanced and are worth diving into as a next step, once you've completed this book.

THE ZODIAC

There are 12 zodiac signs, each named for a constellation in the night sky. The zodiac is based on the ecliptic, an imaginary line that traces the sun's apparent path around the Earth over the course of one year. Ancient astrologers divided this circular path into 12 equal sectors, assigning each the name of the primary constellation present in the sector.

The sun spends approximately one month in each sector, or "sign" of the zodiac, while the moon takes only a few days to move from one sign to the next. Each of the planets has its own unique orbit around the ecliptic, and may spend a few weeks to more than two decades in a sign, depending on its distance from the sun.

Each zodiac sign has distinct energies which manifest as personality traits and qualities in individuals born during the Sun's time in that part of the sky. Each sign also has one or more "ruling" planets, with their own qualities, traits, and energies that correspond with those of the sign. We will examine the zodiac signs in detail in Chapter 3.

THE ELEMENTS

You may have heard of, or even worked with, the four elements fire, earth, air, and water. The elements are said to the basic components of our universe, and they are also basic components in astrology.

Each of the four elements shows a certain type of energy: fire is energized and passionate, earth is grounding and sensual, air is adaptable and thoughtful, and water is receptive and emotional. Each sign of the zodiac is assigned one of these elements, as its characteristics influence the basic traits of the sign. We will review the four elements and their relationship to astrology and magic in Chapter 1.

MODALITIES

Modalities are another building block in the astrological makeup. The modalities are the ways that the signs direct their energy. There are three modalities among the signs:

- **Cardinal signs** are all about initiative and beginnings. These signs are at the beginning of the seasons: Aries (spring), Cancer (summer), Libra (autumn), and Capricorn (winter). Cardinal signs love to try new projects and can sometimes lose steam before they complete those projects. They are go-getters, purposeful, driven, impatient, and can sometimes be a little bit forceful.

- **Fixed signs** are all about stability, order, and resolution. These are the signs in the middle of the seasons and are Taurus (spring), Leo (summer), Scorpio (autumn), and Aquarius (winter). Fixed signs are known to be reliable, loyal, and responsible. They are always seeking out stability and can sometimes be stubborn in their pursuit of concentrated work.

- **Mutable signs** are all about flexibility and change. These signs are at the end of the seasons and are Gemini (spring), Virgo (summer), Sagittarius (autumn), and Pisces (winter). The Mutable signs are known to be versatile, fleeting, and lovers of motion. While they can be thoughtful and witty, they can easily fall into feeling impatient.

PLANETS AND CELESTIAL BODIES

The planets and other celestial bodies above us were associated by the ancients with specific deities who had distinct energetic qualities, personality traits, and behaviors as demonstrated in cultural myths. The planets that bear their names are imbued with these characteristics, and their movements through the zodiac, as well as their relationships to each other, impact people and events on Earth. These energies can also be utilized in magic.

Astrologically speaking, the planets include our two "luminaries"—the Sun and Moon—along with dwarf planets and asteroids. (Note that because the sun and moon don't have proper names like the rest of the celestial bodies, they are not capitalized in standard English. However, when discussed in the context of their astrological energies, the words "sun" and "moon" will be capitalized in this book.) We will examine the planets and celestial bodies in Chapters 2, 4, and 5.

YOUR NATAL CHART

Your natal chart is a snapshot of the astrological energies in the universe at the exact moment you were born. Specifically, it shows you where each planet and luminary was in its journey around the sun from the perspective of Earth, as well as where they were in relation to each other.

The natal chart contains an enormous amount of information about your personality, including the strengths and challenges of your character, and the lessons you're likely to work with in this life. The most significant data points that astrologers work with are your "Big Three," your twelve houses, and any significant aspects between planets at the moment of your birth.

The Big Three

As mentioned earlier, your "Big Three" refers to three major placements within your chart, which are said to collectively reveal an accurate (but not complete) depiction of your personality. These placements are your Sun sign, Moon sign, and Rising sign.

The Sun sign is the most common one we think of when it comes to reading horoscopes. It represents your basic identity, showing how your personality and behavior express in the outside world. The Moon sign is your internal world, ruling over your feelings and influencing how you find comfort and peace. Finally, the Rising sign, which is the sign of the zodiac that was on the eastern horizon when you were born, represents how you appear to the world. Some people say the Sun sign is the actor, while the Rising sign is the mask the actor wears. We will examine the meanings of the "Big Three" in Chapter 3 as we examine each zodiac sign.

The Twelve Houses

An astrological chart is displayed as a circle, divided into 12 different areas, known as "houses." These 12 houses represent various areas of the human experience, such as health, career, family, and relationships.

Your Rising sign determines the placement of your first house, which relates to your identity and how you show yourself to the world. When a significant astrological event occurs, the effects are felt in the area(s) of life governed by the corresponding house. The astrological houses are beyond the scope of this book, but are worth exploring on your own or through a professional astrological reading.

Aspects

Aspects describe a number of ways in which planets connect to or relate to each other within the chart, from the perspective of geometry. Aspects are determined by how many degrees apart two planets are from each other. These spatial relationships are like a conversation between planets, and depending on the angles, they can be beneficial or challenging.

The beneficial aspects are trines (120 degrees apart), and sextiles (60 degrees apart). The challenging aspects are oppositions (180 degrees apart) and squares (90 degrees apart). Conjunctions, when two planets are in the same sign, can be either beneficial or challenging, depending on the energies of the planets themselves. Aspects are beyond the scope of this book, but are worth exploring on your own or through a professional astrological reading.

CONNECTING WITH THE HEAVENS (A MEDITATION)

Now that we've briefly covered the basic elements of astrology, the remainder of this book will dive into the details. The following chapters offer information to help you understand yourself on a deeper level, and learn to utilize the energies of the planets and stars in your magic. First, however, let's take a pause to connect intuitively—rather than just intellectually—to the astrological wisdom we're exploring.

The goal of this meditation is to awaken inspiration by connecting you to the stars and celestial bodies of the heavens. You may read over this meditation and then close your eyes and move through what you recall reading, or you can record yourself reading the meditation and listen. Or you can even read the passage slowly, using your mind's eye to visualize the meditative journey in vivid detail. You may want to research the constellation that your Sun sign is named for and familiarize yourself with its appearance before you begin.

Begin by finding a private and comfortable area where you can work through this meditation without distraction. This may be a favorite spot in your garden, a soft pad of grass under a tree in a park, or curled up on your couch with lit candles and burning incense.

Close your eyes and visualize a safe place in nature that you love. This can be a trail in your favorite nature preserve, the end of a pier overlooking the ocean, or any place with natural beauty and serene energy. Notice how comfortable you feel here, and take a moment to be thankful for the beauty in the world around you.

Begin to slow down your breath, paying close attention to breathing deeply in and slowly releasing the breath. Breathe in and fill your belly. Now slowly breathe out, feeling the warmth of the air leave your body. As you breathe in, envision a sparkling white light emanating from your heart. Each time you breathe in, envision this white light growing, to surround you and protect your energetic field.

Envision this white light sparkling, as the stars of the night sky sparkle. In your mind's eye, look above your body and see that the sparkling stars allow you to access the sky above you. Deeply observe the night sky with wonder and awe. Take a moment to see if you notice a favorite constellation, planet, or even the Moon. How does it feel to admire the sky? Do you see any other images in particular, or hear any messages at this moment?

Next, feel yourself gently floating into the heavens, as you are drawn to the constellation that represents your Sun sign. Look at the stars in this constellation shining and twinkling, their light filling you with warmth and magic.

Take a moment to ask the stars if there are any messages you need to know before embarking on your journey into astrology and the magical stories of the heavens. Listen for their wisdom.

After you have received this message, thank the stars. Take a moment to look at the sky one last time and ask the heavens to fill you with divine light that awakens you to the wisdom and potential within astrology. See if there is a gift, sign, or message just for you that will inform your astrological journey going forward.

Return to focusing on your breath, paying close attention to breathing deeply into your body. As you breathe out, start to envision your body becoming heavy. With each breath out, feel your body descending back to the ground. You realize you have returned to the safe place in nature that you love.

Take moment to slowly move your fingers and toes, stretch your neck, and yawn. When you are ready open your eyes.

Chapter One:
THE ELEMENTS: THE MAGIC AND ASTROLOGY OF FIRE, EARTH, AIR, AND WATER

In the fifth century BCE, Greek philosopher Empedocles of Acragas developed the theory that all matter contained four elements: fire, earth, air, and water. You may already be familiar with the four elements through magical work, or even through working with Tarot, two practices that incorporate the elements.

According to Skye Alexander in *Magickal Astrology*, "The four elements are essential ingredients in the practice of magick as well as astrology." In astrology, the four elements can reveal a person's fundamental personality traits and give a broad overview of their astrological makeup.

The same characteristics of the four elements can also be applied to directing energy and intention in magic. Because of the fundamental role the elements play, we will begin our journey into magical astrology by examining their properties and magical energies.

THE ELEMENT OF FIRE

Rub your hands together quickly. Now slowly move them away from each other, noticing the warm and tingly energy pulsing between your palms. Think about how it feels when you drink a hot cup of tea in the morning. Does the heat fill you with comfort and energy?

Or, perhaps you eat too much wasabi with a piece of sushi—how does the burst of spice feel in your nose? Consider an intense workout you've had. Maybe you had to climb several flights of stairs, or you participated in a 5K. How did your body feel once heated up? Was there something satisfying to completing the task? Or, think about a time you had a creative project you were excited to work on. How did the inspiration feel within you, and how did it motivate you to get the project done?

The element of fire is all about passion, expansion, empowerment, and change. It is about creative inspiration, encouragement that invigorates ambition, and the energy to put yourself out into the world. Fire activates life and is the spark of creation. The flame of fire has illuminated the world around us, been a centerpiece for storytelling, and has created a space where we can cook and heal. It has also been a force of destruction, its chaotic energy igniting fires that destroy homes and burn living beings. Fire has the power to create and the power to devastate.

FIRE IN ASTROLOGY

The zodiac signs associated with fire are Aries, Leo, and Sagittarius. Fire signs are said to be passionate, bossy, outgoing, creative, and enthusiastic. They can be charming, energetic, and confident. Fire signs take care of themselves and have an independent streak.

While they can be fun, bold, and spontaneous, they can also have difficulty completing long term tasks. They are courageous and forceful and must learn how to calm anger and cool down every now and then. We love fire signs for their exciting nature and optimistic outlook on life, but sometimes can feel wiped out if we can't keep up with them.

FIRE IN MAGIC

Fire energy in magic is said to awaken powers, encourage outcomes, instill energy and confidence, stimulate creativity, and spark passion. If you wish to connect with the element of fire, consider lighting candles in your home, building a bonfire, eating a spicy meal, going for a run, or going to a hot yoga session.

In terms of magical tools, the wand, an instrument used to direct energy, is connected to the element of fire. Because of fire's association with metal crafting and the forge, swords and daggers are often associated with the element of fire as well. Those who want to represent fire on their altars may utilize a wand, but can also light a candle or honor the element at their fireplace.

FIRE CORRESPONDENCES

- **Zodiac Signs:** Aries, Leo, Sagittarius
- **Magical Associations:** ambition, confidence, creativity, endurance, energy, inspiration, optimism, passion, transformation, willpower
- **Plants, Herbs, Resins, and Essential Oils:** allspice, angelica, basil, bay, black pepper, carnation, cedarwood, cinnamon, clove, copal, dragon's blood, frankincense, galangal, garlic, ginger, ginseng, hibiscus, lime, juniper, neroli, nutmeg, oak, orange, rosemary, saffron, tobacco
- **Crystals and Metals:** amber, brass, carnelian, citrine, fire agate, flint, garnet, gold, iron, opal, pyrite, rainbow obsidian, red jasper, ruby, sardonyx, shungite, sunstone, tangerine quartz, topaz
- **Tarot cards:** the suit of Wands
- **Colors:** red, orange, gold
- **Mythical Creatures of Fire:** dragon, phoenix, salamanders, sphinx
- **Sacred Locations with Fire Energy:** Chaco Canyon, Devils Tower, Fire of Kildare, Giza Plateau, Mauna Loa, Nazca Lines, Petra, Sedona, Temple of Vesta, Uluru, Valley of the Kings. Any place you find sacred that is arid and dry has fire energy.

FIRE OIL BLEND

Wear this oil blend when you are looking to bring the magic of the fire element into your life. You can also wear this during Aries, Leo, and Sagittarius seasons to boost your mood and energy. This is also a helpful blend to wear during Mars Retrograde, which we'll discuss in Chapter 5.

As with any essential oil blend, be mindful if you have sensitive skin or allergies, and do not ingest internally.

You will need:

- 4-dram glass vial
- Small funnel (optional)
- Carrier oil (for fire, olive oil is recommended)
- 9 drops dragon's blood oil
- 9 drops frankincense oil
- 6 drops carnation oil
- 6 drops orange oil
- 6 drops neroli oil
- Optional: carnelian and pyrite crystal chips
- Optional: dried hibiscus and sunflower petals

Instructions:

Add the drops of oil to the glass vial. If you have crystal chips and/or dried petals, feel free to add a small amount of each. Slowly start to fill the glass vial with the carrier oil. (You may wish to use a funnel for this step.)

When it is about ¾ full, put the cap on the vial and very gently swirl to blend the oils together. Remove the cap and test the fragrance – this is your special blend, so add more of any of the above oils one drop at a time if you would like to modify the scent.

When the adjustments are finished, add more carrier oil to the glass vial, leaving a little room at the top, and tightly seal. Note that carrier oils do have a shelf life—olive oil can last up to about two years.

FIRE CANDLE SPELL FOR CONFIDENCE

This is a supportive spell for boosting your confidence and self-esteem. You can do this spell whenever you need to, but if you wish to magically time it with astrology, perform this spell on a Sunday or when the Moon is in Aries, Leo, or Sagittarius.

If you haven't made the Fire Oil blend above, you can substitute with frankincense essential oil.

You will need:

- Red spell candle
- A piece of carnelian
- Fire Oil blend (or frankincense oil)
- Red ribbon
- Small piece of paper and red pen

Instructions:

Begin by dressing the red spell candle with the Fire Oil blend. Place the candle in a fire safe holder and light.

On the piece of paper, write down three words you would use to define confidence. Next to those three words, write down three words you would use to describe how confidence feels. Finally, next to those three words, write down three words you would use to explain the *results* of confidence.

Now, envision yourself exhibiting all these characteristics of confidence. Visualize these feelings happening within you in a specific moment. Really pause to feel and experience confidence in your mind's eye. What are you wearing, and where are you? Do you feel more expressive? More decisive? More courageous? Hold this vision and this feeling for as long as you can.

When you feel ready, take the carnelian and wrap it in the paper. Now wrap the ribbon around the paper. Knot it once and recite: "*I am confident because I am brilliant.*"

Wrap the ribbon around the crystal again. Knot it again and recite: "*I respond with confidence because I am inspired.*"

Wrap the ribbon around the crystal one more time. Knot it again and recite: "*I live with confidence because I am worthy of confidence.*"

Hold the crystal in your hand and consider the words you wrote on the paper and the vision you had of yourself earlier. Then leave the crystal beside the candle, allowing the candle to burn completely down. Carry the wrapped crystal with you whenever you need to access the energy of confidence.

THE ELEMENT OF EARTH

Lie flat on the ground, allowing gravity to anchor you to the earth – how does it feel with your body securely supported by the ground? Think about the sensations you experience when you walk barefoot on the grass, or sink your hands into the dirt in your garden.

Is there something familiar and healing about these actions? Consider a time you had a hearty dinner with friends and family, one that was filling, satisfying, and full of nutrients. Did you feel gratitude for the abundance in your life in those moments? Or can you remember a time you managed a plan at your work that successfully brought you a promotion or bonus? What did that prosperity feel like and how did it help you?

The element of earth is all about manifestation, practicality, stability, and the physical form. It is all about growth and experience in our material world, governing our physical bodies as well as rocks, plants, and even the present moment. When we think of the earth we are taken to a lush and verdant place of growth and abundance.

Perhaps you have a favorite hike in the woods by your home, or you feel instantly healed when you cuddle with your pet. Or you experience an immense feeling of gratitude when you look at the beauty of nature around you. Earth energy is a potent combination of healing, growth, comfort, security, and embracing the abundance in nature.

EARTH IN ASTROLOGY

The astrological signs associated with earth are Taurus, Virgo, and Capricorn. Earth signs are known as being dependable, stable, practical, and grounding. They have a love for beauty and love to be surrounded by attractive things.

Earth signs are known to be hard workers, and their success allows them to enjoy prosperity, comfort, luxury, and splendor. We love how realistic and dependable earth signs can be, but we sometimes get frustrated at their stubbornness.

EARTH IN MAGIC

Earth energy supports spells associated with wellness, healing, fertility, grounding, prosperity, and abundance. If you wish to connect with the element of earth, consider going for a hike in the woods, tending a house plant or small garden, grounding by walking barefoot in the grass, spending time with your pets, working with clay in a ceramics class, or getting a relaxing massage.

In terms of magical tools, the pentacle, which is shaped like a star enclosed within a circle, is connected to the element of earth. When used on Wiccan altars, the pentacle is often depicted on an engraved disc made of wood, clay, stone, or metal. Sometimes a painting or image of a pentacle is used. You can also have a small dish of salt and/or soil to represent earth.

EARTH CORRESPONDENCES

- **Zodiac Signs:** Taurus, Virgo, Capricorn

- **Magical Associations:** abundance, comfort, fertility, grounding, growth, healing, home blessings, manifestation, protection, prosperity, security, stability

- **Plants, Herbs, Resins, and Essential Oils:** amber, beets, carrots, cinquefoil, cotton, cypress, fir, grass, honeysuckle, mugwort, oakmoss, patchouli, tea tree, vetiver, walnut

- **Crystals:** alexandrite, black tourmaline, brown jasper, coal, emerald, fossils, green aventurine, green jade, hematite, jet, lodestone, malachite, moss agate, obsidian, peridot, petrified wood, palo santo, pyrite, smoky quartz, tiger's eye

- **Tarot card:** the suit of Pentacles

- **Colors:** green, brown

- **Mythical Creatures of Earth:** dwarves, gnomes, hobbits, sasquatch

- **Sacred Locations with Earth Energy:** Angkor Wot, Appalachian Trail, Black Forest, Bodhi Tree, Cahokia, Central Park, Majorville Cairn and Medicine Wheel, Newgrange, New Zealand, Pacific Northwest, Rainforests, Redwood National Forest, Stonehenge. Any place you find sacred that is green and lush has earth energy.

EARTH OIL BLEND

Wear this oil blend when you are looking to bring the magic of the earth element into your life. You can also wear this during Taurus, Virgo, or Capricorn seasons to boost your mood and energy. This is also a helpful blend to wear during Venus Retrograde, which we'll discuss in Chapter 5.

As with any essential oil blend, be mindful if you have sensitive skin or allergies and do not ingest internally.

You will need:

- 4-dram glass vial
- Small funnel (optional)
- Carrier oil (for earth, jojoba oil is recommended)
- 8 drops oakmoss oil
- 8 drops vetiver oil
- 4 drops patchouli
- 4 drops amber oil
- 2 drops fir needle oil
- Optional: jade and/or emerald crystal chips
- Optional: dried pine needles and/or dried honeysuckle petals

Instructions:

Add the drops of oil to the glass vial. If you have crystal chips and/or dried needles and petals, feel free to add a small amount of each. Slowly start to fill the glass vial with the carrier oil. (You may wish to use a funnel for this step.)

When it is about ¾ full, put the cap on the vial and very gently swirl to blend. Remove the cap and test the fragrance – this is your special blend, so add more of any of the above oils one drop at a time if you would like to modify the scent.

When the adjustments are finished, add more carrier oil to the glass vial, leaving a little room at the top, and tightly seal. Note that carrier oils do have a shelf life—jojoba oil can last up to about three years.

EARTH PROSPERITY COIN PURSE

This is a fun little money spell for inviting energies of prosperity into your life. You can do this spell when you need to, but if you wish to magically time it with astrology, perform this spell on a Sunday or Thursday, when the Moon is in Taurus, Virgo, or Capricorn.

If you haven't made the Earth Oil blend above, you can substitute with patchouli essential oil.

You will need:

- A small coin purse
- A piece of green jade
- A piece of aventurine
- Earth Oil blend

- Optional: a pinch of cinquefoil blended with a drop of Earth Oil blend
- Lucky coin
- Largest bill of currency you can spare ($1 is absolutely okay to use)
- Green pen

Instructions:

Take the bill and anoint it with the Earth Oil blend or patchouli oil at the corners and the center on both sides. When it's dry, you are going to write an incantation on the borders of the bill with the green pen, doing the best you can to write in one continuous loop without lifting the pen. It's okay if it doesn't look perfect! Write the following incantation:

"I have immense financial prosperity. A beautiful abundance of money flows into my life with ease. Prosperity and success come to me naturally."

Take the bill, along with the crystals, lucky coin, and cinquefoil, if using, and put it into the coin purse. Hold the coin purse and close your eyes. Envision the purse glowing gold, feeling heavier and heavier as it fills with more and more money. Take a moment to visualize yourself with incredible wealth. Do not limit yourself with what you see as possible—just enjoy where your hopes and dreams take you.

Say the incantation above out loud, three times. Put the coin purse in your pocket, place of business, or purse, and carry it with you as much as possible. If you find lucky coins or trinkets, feel free to add them to the coin purse as well—since the spell is meant to help prosperity grow, the contents of the coin purse can grow as well!

THE ELEMENT OF AIR

Take a long, slow, deep breath through your nose. Feel the air fill your lungs and belly. Hold the air in your body for a few extra seconds and then slowly release the breath through your mouth. Did the air feel cool entering your body and warm exiting your body? Did you feel a little more relaxed or at ease after the deep breathing?

Now, consider your favorite song, or soothing sounds like wind chimes, ocean waves, or meditation music. How do you respond when you hear those sounds? Have you ever repeated a mantra or an incantation? How did that practice affect your state of mind? Have you spoken a prayer or an intention out loud? What did you ask for and did your request come into fruition? Consider something you love to learn about. How does it feel to research and discover new information about the subject?

The element of air is all about communication, thought, intelligence, expansion, and adaptability. Air is invisible, yet it surrounds us and is in constant motion. Air is about considering options, making decisions, and acting on them. It governs wisdom, writing, and the future. Through air we think, speak, and bring ideas to life. If we are in balance with this element, our mental space can give us the opportunity to feel wise and enlightened.

AIR IN ASTROLOGY

The astrological signs associated with air are Gemini, Libra, and Aquarius. Air signs are known as being thoughtful, social, smart, and flexible. Air signs have brilliant ideas but can also be indecisive, perhaps because they're so good at observing everything and seeing viable options everywhere.

We love to have long, meaningful conversations with air signs, but can sometimes feel hurt when they come off as aloof or emotionally distant.

AIR IN MAGIC

Air energy supports wisdom, inspiration, communication, studying, and making choices. It can help us see things clearly and make smart decisions. If you wish to connect with the element of air, consider writing a poem, meditating, repeating a mantra, singing, hanging a dreamcatcher in your room, admiring the clouds in the sky or admiring the stars at night, doing breathwork, going to a sound healing session, or browsing your favorite used bookstore.

In terms of magical tools, the athame, a ritual knife that is often used to cast circles and direct energy, is connected to the element of air. Those who want to represent air on their altars can use a feather or burn incense (the smoke represents air). Bells and chimes are also aligned to the magic of air, and simply singing or chanting wishes is very airy in nature as well! Since the element of air is aligned with knowledge, books, journals, and grimoires can also represent air.

AIR CORRESPONDENCES

- **Zodiac Signs:** Gemini, Libra, Aquarius
- **Magical Associations:** action, clarity, communication, direction, enlightenment, focus, insight, intellectualism, intelligence, learning, mental agility, observation, perception, public speaking, riddles, teaching, travel, wisdom, writing
- **Plants, Herbs, Resins, and Essential Oils:** anise, Arabic gum, aster, benzoin, bergamot, chicory, clary sage, dandelion, eucalyptus, eyebright, fennel, fern, hazel, lavender, lemongrass, lemon verbena, lilac, lily of the valley, marjoram, mastic gum, mint, mistletoe, parsley, peppermint, rue-anemone flower, rosemary, star anise, thyme, witch hazel, yarrow
- **Crystals and metals:** aluminum, angelite, apophyllite, celestite, crystal quartz, danburite, fluorite, howlite, labradorite, lepidolite, lithium quartz, mica, moldavite, selenite, tin, tourmalated quartz
- **Tarot cards:** the suit of Swords
- **Colors:** yellow, white, silver
- **Mythical Creatures of Air:** elves, faeries, Pegasus, sylphs, wil'o'wisps
- **Sacred Locations with Air Energy:** the Alps, Al-Qarawiyyin Library, Asheville, NC, Boulder, CO, Glastonbury Tor, Machu Picchu, Mount Everest or

other high peaks, Mount Shasta, Nepal, Oxford University, Patagonia, Sears Tower and skyscrapers, Sorbonne University, Tibet, Any place you find sacred that is breezy and/or high in elevation has air energy.

AIR OIL BLEND

Wear this oil blend when you are looking to bring the magic of the air element into your life. You can also wear this during Gemini, Libra, and Aquarius seasons to boost your mood and energy. This is also a helpful blend to wear during Mercury Retrograde, which we'll discuss in Chapter 5.

As with any essential oil blend, be mindful if you have sensitive skin or allergies and do not ingest internally.

You will need:

- 4-dram glass vial
- Small funnel (optional)
- Carrier oil (for air, sweet almond oil is recommended)
- 9 drops lavender oil
- 7 drops bergamot oil
- 3 drops clary sage oil
- 3 drops rosemary oil
- 2 drops eucalyptus oil
- Optional: crystal quartz and fluorite chips
- Optional: dandelion seeds and dried lavender herbs

Instructions:

Add the drops of oil to the glass vial. If you have crystal chips, dandelion seeds, and/or dried lavender, feel free to add a small amount of each. Slowly start to fill the glass vial with the carrier oil. (You may wish to use a funnel for this step.)

When it is about ¾ full, put the cap on the vial and very gently swirl to blend the oils together. Remove the cap and test the fragrance – this is your special blend, so add more of any of the above oils one drop at a time if you would like to modify the scent.

When the adjustments are finished, add more carrier oil to the glass vial, leaving a little room at the top, and tightly seal. Note that carrier oils do have a shelf life—sweet almond oil can last up to about two years.

WINDY WISHING SPELL

This spell is a simple one to try out when you have a wish you'd like to send out into the universe. You can do this spell when you need to, but if you wish to magically time it with astrology, perform this spell on a Wednesday, or when the Moon is in Gemini, Libra, or Aquarius.

You will need:

- A mixing bowl
- Dandelion seeds (from one or two dandelions)
- 1 tsp. fennel seeds
- 1 tsp. lavender herbs
- 1 tsp. thyme herbs
- Optional: crystal quartz

Instructions:

Mix all the herbs and seeds in the mixing bowl. Place the mixed contents in a bag with the crystal quartz. Take the bag to a high lookout point or a windy location where you will have privacy. Hold the bag in your hands and consider the wish you would like to have granted. What would really help you right now? Use your mind's eye to see the results of having that wish granted.

Take a moment to take deep, slow breaths, feeling the air move through your body. Say the following incantation:

"Air moves through me, magic flows on the breeze. May divinity in the sky hear my wish and support me. My wish is: (say your wish)."

Take a small handful of the ingredients from your bag and blow it into the wind. Repeat this three times.

THE ELEMENT OF WATER

Get yourself a glass of water. Slowly take a sip. How does the water feel in your mouth? How does it feel as you swallow it and it moves down in your belly? Think about a time you dove into a body of cool, refreshing water. How about the last time you treated yourself to a long, hot shower? How did your body respond to the feeling of the water moving around you in these instances?

Consider a moment you were overwhelmed with emotion. Perhaps you watched a romantic movie and cried at the moment the two lovers kissed, or you attended a funeral and wept with grief. How was the crying beneficial to you? Have you ever had a dream that felt so real you had trouble believing it happened while you were sleeping? Have you ever had a psychic premonition in a dream?

The element of water is all about emotions, empathy, receptivity, and intuition. Water governs over everything in liquid form, including natural bodies of water, rain, potable drinks, potions, and oils. Our bodies are made of about 60% water, so we need water in order to survive. Water quenches our thirst, cleanses our bodies and homes, and is transformed into a sacred liquid by priests and priestesses in religions around the world. Water also governs the past.

WATER IN ASTROLOGY

The astrological signs associated with water are Cancer, Scorpio, and Pisces. Water signs are deep, emotional, compassionate, and intuitive. They are psychic sponges, picking up on the feelings of the people and places around them.

They are known to be mysterious and sensitive. While we love how much they make us feel loved, we can be put off by their clinginess or tendency to be moody.

WATER IN MAGIC

Water energy supports our sensitive traits, helping us to honor and deepen our psychic abilities, our intuition, and our connection to the Otherworld. Water energy in magic can also help us explore romance, peacefulness, relaxation, and going with the flow. If you wish to connect with the element of water, consider taking a salt bath, visiting the ocean, going for a swim, working with aromatherapy, enjoying a comforting cup of tea, meditating by a waterfall, or getting a reiki session.

In terms of tools, the chalice, a sacred cup that is often used to hold wine or water in ritual, is connected to the element of water. Those who wish to represent water on their altar can do so with a vessel full of water, oceanic items such as shells and sea glass, or a potion bottle.

WATER CORRESPONDENCES

- **Zodiac Signs:** Cancer, Scorpio, Pisces

- **Magical Associations:** ancestral work, compassion, divination, dreams, emotional healing, empathy, forgiveness, intuition, love, romance, peace, psychic abilities, ocean magic, weather magic

- **Plants, Herbs, Resins and Essential oils:** aloe, apple, camphor, catnip, coconut, cucumber, elderberry, gardenia, geranium, heather, iris, jasmine, lemon, lemon balm, lily, lobelia, lotus, myrrh, passionflower, peach, plumeria, rose, sandalwood, sweet pea, tansy, tonka beans, tuberose, vanilla, violet, willow, ylang-ylang

- **Crystals:** amethyst, aquamarine, azurite, blue calcite, blue chalcedony, blue kyanite, blue lace agate, blue topaz, chrysocolla, lapis lazuli, larimar, moonstone, pearl, rose quartz, sodalite, turquoise

- **Tarot cards:** the suit of Cups

- **Colors:** blue, purple

- **Mythical Creatures of Water:** kelpie, mermaids, Nessie, nymphs, selkies, sirens

- **Sacred Locations with Water Energy:** Atlantis, Avalon, Bath, Blue Holes, Bimini, Brigid's Well, Chalice Well, Crater Lake, Ganges River, Great Barrier Reef, the Great Lakes, Lake Geneva, Lake Tahoe, Lake Titicaca, Lemuria, Mississippi River, Niagara Falls, Nile River, Orkney Island, the Sacred Cenote at Chichen Itza, Salt Lake, Sardinia, Taj Mahal, Tulum.

Any place you find sacred that is near a body of water has water energy.

WATER OIL BLEND

Wear this oil blend when you are looking to bring the magic of the water element into your life. You can also wear this during Cancer, Scorpio, and Pisces seasons to boost your mood and energy. This is also a helpful blend to wear during Venus Retrograde, which we'll discuss in Chapter 5.

As with any essential oil blend, be mindful if you have sensitive skin or allergies and do not ingest internally.

You will need:

- 4-dram glass vial
- Small funnel (optional)
- Carrier oil (for water, fractionated coconut oil is recommended)
- 9 drops vanilla
- 9 drops sandalwood
- 6 drops gardenia
- 5 drops jasmine
- 1 drop rose or ylang-ylang
- Optional: aquamarine and lapis lazuli chips
- Optional: 1 tonka bean and dried lemon peel

Instructions:

Add the drops of oil to the glass vial. If you're using crystal chips, a tonka bean, and/or dried lemon peel, feel free to add a small amount of each. Slowly start to fill the glass vial with the carrier oil. (You may wish to use a funnel for this step.)

When it is about ¾ full, put the cap on the vial and very gently swirl to blend the oils together. Remove the cap and test the fragrance – this is your special blend, so add more of any of the above oils one drop at a time if you would like to modify the scent.

When the adjustments are finished, add more carrier oil to the glass vial, leaving a little room at the top, and tightly seal. Note that carrier oils do have a shelf life—fractionated coconut oil can last up to about five years.

SCRYING BOWL FOR VISIONS

Scrying is a form of divination where you gaze into a reflective surface to catch glimpses of images that can be interpreted as symbols, omens, or psychic messages. You may be familiar with the archetypal image of the psychic gazing deeply into a crystal ball. However, scrying can be done in any reflective surface, including lakes, bird baths, mirrors, and bowls filled with water.

The best time to do this spell is at dusk or in the early evening, especially during a full moon or on a Monday. This would also be excellent to try during the Beltane season in May, or the Samhain season in October, when it is believed that psychic senses are heightened.

The sea salt is optional, but is meant to act as a protective boundary. You can scatter sea salt around the area you are working, or keep a handful of the salt in your pocket. If you prefer something you don't need to clean up later, visualize white light glowing around you and protecting you from harm or unwanted energy. If you haven't made the Water Oil blend above, you can substitute with jasmine essential oil.

You will need:

- Sea salt (optional)
- A dark-colored, shallow, wide bowl
- Water
- Black ink
- Water Oil blend
- 2 purple spell candles

Instructions:

Place the bowl at a clean tabletop in front of where you will be seated. Pour water into the bowl. Add black ink, one drop at a time, until the water is completely black. Light the two candles and place them to the left and right of the bowl, positioned so that the light creates a flicking motion on the surface of the water.

Dim the lights (or turn them off) and drop a few drops of the Water Oil blend into the bowl. Make yourself comfortable and lean over the surface of the bowl. Allow your focus to go fuzzy, as if you are softening your gaze. See if you notice and colors or images in the water's surface.

Even if you don't see anything, you may *sense* something or receive psychic messages in another way—for example, through a clairaudient message. You may feel dreamy or sleepy from doing this, and that's okay. Try it out for a few minutes at first, and gradually increase the amount of time you spend scrying as you develop your practice.

When you are done, take your time getting up and moving around. You may want to stretch, take a few deep breaths, or have a small snack. Take a moment to write down whatever messages you received or images you saw. If you are feeling adventurous, consider pouring the wax from the candles into the bowl, and interpret the shape that the wax makes when it cools.

ELEMENTAL CARD SPREAD

There are many variations of elemental spreads for divination purposes. This particular spread is meant to help you see how the elements are currently guiding you. This spread can be used with Tarot or oracle cards, but can also be used with other divination tools such as runes or crystal divination kits.

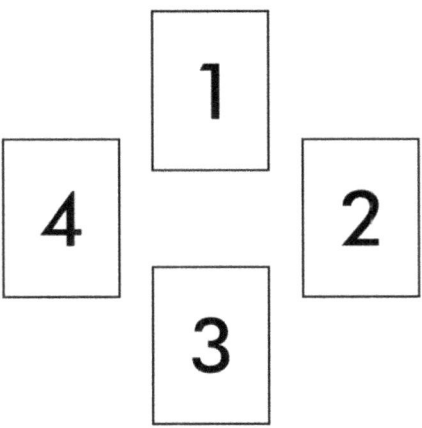

- **Card one** represents the element of earth. This card reveals what is stabilizing for you currently. It can guide you to what will bring security and prosperity in your life.

- **Card two** represents the element of air. This card reveals what is taking up the most time in your thoughts right now. It can guide you to what needs to be focused on or researched in your life.

- **Card three** represents the element of fire. This card reveals what is inspiring you currently. It can guide you to ways to bring more excitement, creativity, and passion in your life.

- **Card four** represents the element of water. This card reveals what is influencing your emotions currently. It can guide you to ways to feeling more peace and how to awaken your psychic talents.

EXPERIENCING THE ELEMENTS IN YOUR BODY (A MEDITATION)

This is a short meditation that you can begin your day with. It will help you remember that all the elements live within you, just as they are the building blocks of the universe. If possible, try this meditation outdoors, allowing any sensory information from the natural world to enhance your experience.

When you are in your safe, private, and comfortable location, close your eyes and bring your attention inwards. Take a deep breath in, recognizing that the element of air is moving through your body. Hold the air in your lungs for a few seconds, and slowly release it through your mouth, knowing your spirit's energy is now laced in the air around you. Appreciate how air lives within you and animates you.

Draw your attention to your body. Are there any places of tension? Take a moment to scan these places and focus on bringing relief to them. Let go of tension you may be holding in your jaw or your neck, or anywhere else. How does it feel to release that tension and experience more ease? Notice how the earth feels beneath you: the element of earth is resonating through you, grounding you to the planet and allowing you the opportunity to feel comfort. Appreciate how earth lives within you and supports you.

Draw your attention to the warmth in your body. Where do you feel heat in your body? Are there places that are cold? If you are feeling comfortable, rub your hands together or breathe into your hands. What does the warmth feel like? Your body generates heat, radiating the element of fire. Allow the spaces of heat in your body to awaken creative ideas. Allow your mind to wander into new ideas that you would like to pursue and act on. Appreciate how fire lives within you and inspires you.

Finally, draw your attention to your mouth. Swallow, feeling liquid going down your throat. If you are comfortable, take your hand and place it over your heart to feel your heartbeat. Your heart is pumping blood through your body, another reminder that your body carries the element of water through it. This element allows you to live and to feel. Appreciate how water lives within you and nourishes you.

When you are ready, slowly bring yourself back to the present moment and complete the meditation by opening your eyes.

Chapter Two:
PLANET POWER: THE MAGIC AND ASTROLOGY OF CELESTIAL BODIES

In this chapter, we will review the astrological and magical influences of the celestial bodies within our solar system. In traditional astrology, these celestial bodies include the planets and the luminaries—the Sun and Moon. Modern astrology also incorporates several known dwarf planets, planetoids, and even asteroids that were not discovered until very recently. These will be discussed briefly toward the end of the chapter.

Before the invention of the telescope, there were five known planets: Mercury, Venus, Mars, Jupiter, and Saturn. The sun and moon were also considered planets. (Earth wasn't considered a planet, as it was thought for millennia to be the center of the universe that all celestial bodies revolved around.)

These planets had different names across ancient cultures, but were typically named for important deities in each culture's pantheon. Some ancients believed the planets were themselves deities, while others named them for deities to honor the power and influence they observed in these celestial bodies.

The English names for these ancient planets are borrowed from the Roman names, with the exception of Venus, which comes from the Greeks. As new planets were being discovered, it was agreed upon by astronomers at the time to continue the tradition of naming them for Greek and Roman deities.

Today, the names for newly discovered planets and other celestial bodies are determined by the International Astronomical Union (IAU), and the tradition has expanded to borrowing from other cultures throughout the world, as we will see in the section "Other Celestial Bodies," below.

For people new to astrology, it may seem random to simply ascribe the energetic traits of the planets to the deities they were named for—especially the "modern" planets of Uranus, Neptune, and Pluto, which were named by astronomers rather than ancient mystics. However, these planetary energies are universal, and their influences on Earth have been consistently observed by both ancient and modern astrologers.

As we will see below, the modern planets were discovered during periods of history that reflect the dominant energies of the planets themselves. Whether or not the namers of these planets paid any attention to astrology, the names they chose were perfect fits.

Your natal chart will show where each of these celestial bodies was positioned in the sky at the moment of your birth. Each will be within a specific zodiac sign. (If you haven't yet accessed your chart, now is a good time to do so—see the Introduction for tips on how to do this.) This is what people are referring to when they say things like, "My Venus is in Leo," or "My Mercury is in Gemini."

To get a better understanding of your astrological makeup, you can examine the meaning of the planets in this chapter and then compare them with the meanings of the signs in the following chapter.

THE SUN

As the source of light (and therefore life) on Earth, the sun was worshiped by ancient cultures around the world, and is still central to many modern pagan religions. Even before it was understood that the Earth orbits the sun and not the other way around, the sun's central role to human survival was clear.

The ancient Greeks called the sun Helios, after the god who drove a fiery chariot across the sky each day to provide the world with light. The Romans called the sun "Sol" (which is where we get the word "solar") after their god Sol Invictus (meaning "invincible"), whose light dispelled the forces of evil.

In astrology, the Sun represents who you know yourself to be. Its placement in your natal chart influences your identity, how you see yourself, your innate potential, and your purpose in life. Just as the light and heat of the sun can feel pleasant, inadequate, or overwhelming, depending on the circumstances, the attributes of each Sun sign can sometimes be faint, and at other times come on too strong for our own best interests, or the interests of others.

Understanding more about how our Sun sign influences our personality can help us to become the best versions of ourselves we can be. We will discuss the role of the Sun sign again in Chapter 3.

THE SUN IN MAGIC

We work with the energy of the Sun to bring warmth and confidence into our lives, revitalize projects, encourage success, illuminate our path, and awaken growth. If you want to align with the energy of the Sun, consider going for a walk on a sunny day, using a sun lamp, drinking tea soaked in sun rays, wearing gold, enjoying a fire, or following solar flare activity.

The deities of the Sun, such as Bast, Sekhmet, Sol, Helios, Apollo, Ra, Lugh, Vishnu, Shiva, and Horus, show assertive, powerful, and almighty energy.

SUN CORRESPONDENCES

- **Magical Associations:** activation, confidence, empowerment, growth, healing, illumination, success, masculinity, realizing potential, vitality

- **Plants, Herbs, Resins and Essential Oils:** angelica, bay, calendula, carnation, cinnamon, copal, daffodil, frankincense, gum Arabic, heliotrope, juniper, mistletoe, neroli, oak, orange, rosemary, saffron, St. John's Wort, sunflower

- **Crystals:** carnelian, citrine, Icelandic spar (clear optical calcite), orange calcite, sunstone, tangerine quartz, topaz
- **Foods of the Sun for Nutrition and Strength:** citrus fruit, honey, mango, sunflower seeds
- **Tarot card:** The Sun
- **Colors:** gold, orange, yellow
- **Day of the Week:** Sunday

SUNRISE SPELL FOR ILLUMINATION AND DIRECTION

Norse Sagas spoke of Vikings using a "sunstone" to help navigate on their overseas journeys, much like a compass. It is now believed that this sunstone was Icelandic spar, or clear optical calcite.

By viewing sunlight moving through the crystal, Viking sailors were able determine where the sun was. This calcite has a strong connection to Sun energy for this reason, and is also known to bring clarity to situations, amplify optimism, and help determine a smooth-moving direction to go in. This sunrise spell will help you bring clarity, direction, and optimism to your life. It is especially good to perform if you are feeling bored or stuck in a stagnant phase.

For this simple spell, you will need a piece of Icelandic spar, an early Sunday morning, and a safe and private lookout where you can watch the sunrise. This spell can also be done on either of the solstices.

Go to your lookout location at early dawn before the sun has come up with your Icelandic spar. Quietly take in the horizon, noticing the colors of the sky, any cloud formations, and anything else about the sky that captures your attention. Use this time to take deep breaths and observe your surroundings, as well as how you are feeling. Make a mental note of any intuitive messages you may receive in this quiet, peaceful moment.

As the sun begins to rise, hold up the Icelandic spar, allowing the light to shine through the crystal. Keep holding it up, repeating this incantation:

"I welcome the sunlight into my life. The Sun fills this stone with the magic of the divine. May this sunstone illuminate the right path for me to take, one where hope, inspiration, and happiness are awake."

Repeat this incantation as much as you like. Carry the stone with you, taking it out and holding it up to the sky any time you need divine guidance in directing you towards hope, inspiration, and happiness.

THE MOON

Our other luminary, the Moon, was also revered by the ancients, and was associated with a plethora of deities from various cultures, including the Greek goddesses Selene and Artemis, the Roman goddess Luna (which is where we get the word "lunar"), the Egyptian goddess Isis, and many others. Not all cultures perceived the energies of the moon as exclusively female (it was also associated with the Egyptian god Thoth, for example), but for the purposes of astrology, as well as much of modern paganism, the feminine energies of this celestial body are the focus.

The English word "moon" stems from an ancient word that equates to "month" in many languages, as the relatively short orbit of the moon created a natural way of tracking time. The lunar cycle is also roughly equivalent to the length of the female menstrual cycle, which further underscores the feminine associations with this luminary.

In astrology, as well as in witchcraft, the Moon is associated with the hidden, the shadow, the obscured parts of the human psyche. This makes sense, given that at least part of the moon is hidden in shadow for the vast majority of the lunar cycle. The Moon represents your innermost self, and its placement in your natal chart influences your private feelings, your intuition, your daily habits, and what makes you emotionally comfortable. We will discuss the role of the Moon sign again in Chapter 3.

THE MOON IN MAGIC

We work with the energy of the Moon to awaken our gentle, receptive side. The Moon can assist in magic when you are wanting to feel peace, compassion, restfulness, and comfort.

If you want to align with the energy of the Moon, consider going for a walk under a full moon, attending an Esbat (full moon) ritual, taking a sea salt bath, growing moonflowers in your garden, or reflecting on your moods as you move through the lunar phases. The deities of the Moon, such as Luna, Diana, Selene, Luna, Isis, and Artemis, show receptive and nurturing energy.

MOON CORRESPONDENCES

- **Magical Associations:** compassion, dreamwork, love, ocean magic, peacefulness, psychic awakening, rebirth, rhythm and cycles, sleep and rest, transformation, witchcraft, women's mysteries, working with feminine deities

- **Plants, Herbs, Resins and Essential Oils:** aloe, camphor, coconut, gardenia, jasmine, lemon, lotus, moonwort, myrrh, sandalwood, willow

- **Crystals:** moonstone, morganite, pearl, selenite, white calcite

- **Foods of the Moon for Hydration and Cleansing:** celery, cucumber, grapes, lettuce, melon, mushrooms
- **Tarot Card:** The High Priestess
- **Colors:** pearl, silver
- **Day of the Week:** Monday

MOON BATH SOAK FOR PEACEFULNESS

This soothing and comforting bath soak blend is meant to bring you peace of mind, but also to awaken your psychic abilities, making it an excellent way to end a long day and/or prepare for ritual and magic.

Note that essential oils are called for in this recipe, which you should be mindful of if you have sensitive skin. Also, coconut oil can make for a slippery bathtub, so step carefully and give the tub a good wipe-down after your bath.

You will need:

- 1 to 2 cups whole milk or oat milk
- 2 cups Epsom salts
- 1 tbsp. coconut oil
- 1 tbsp. aloe vera gel
- 13 drops sandalwood essential oil
- 13 drops jasmine essential oil

Directions:

Draw the water and slowly add all the ingredients into the tub.

To heighten this experience, consider lighting candles and adding a piece or two of moonstone to the water before you get in.

MERCURY

Mercury was called Nabu by the Babylonians, after their god of writing and wisdom. The Greeks named this speedy planet after their god Hermes, the winged messenger who would swiftly exchange messages between the gods. Hermes was known to the Romans as Mercury. He carried a caduceus—a staff with two intertwined snakes—which to the Romans symbolized diplomacy and peace. Mercury was a smart, quick-thinking god who ruled over translators, interpreters, communication, and luck. Along with Hermes, deities from other cultures who are associated with Mercury are Thoth, Athena, and Seshat.

In astrology, Mercury represents communication, learning, and travel. In your natal chart, your Mercury placement influences how you communicate your thoughts to others, what you're naturally curious about, how you approach decision-making, and how you deal with anxiety or excess mental energy. Mercury can show you where you communicate the best as well as how to enhance your capacity to focus, think, and learn.

MERCURY IN MAGIC

We work with the energy of Mercury to awaken our intellect, bring us wisdom, help us concentrate, communicate with intention, speak honestly, hear the truth, write eloquently, and travel safely.

If you want to align with the energy of Mercury, consider writing in a journal, writing a letter or sending a card to a friend or family member, planning a trip, listening to thought-provoking podcast, reading a book, or participating in a workshop or class (either as a teacher or a student).

MERCURY CORRESPONDENCES

- **Magical Associations:** intellect, communication, travel, wisdom, study, concentration, swift delivery, travel, Book of Shadows work

- **Plants, Herbs, Resins and Essential Oils:** almond, benzoin, clary sage, dill, fennel, fern, horehound, lavender, lemongrass, marjoram, peppermint, rosemary, spearmint, thyme

- **Crystals:** blue lace agate, cat's eye, fluorite, hematite, muscovite, onyx

- **Foods of Mercury for Detoxification and Cleansing:** almond, beans, chia seeds, dandelion leaf, fennel, flax seed

- **Tarot card:** The Magician

- **Colors:** blue, gray
- **Day of the Week:** Wednesday

MERCURY INCENSE BLEND FOR WISDOM

This incense blend combines loose herbs, resins, and, if you like, a little bit of essential oil. It can be burned safely on a charcoal briquette within a fire safe container (such as a small cast iron cauldron).

Use this incense when you need to awaken your mental abilities; for example, when you are studying, writing, or doing research. You can also burn this during Mercury Retrograde (discussed in Chapter 5) or before traveling.

You will need equal parts of the following:

- Benzoin resin (ground into smaller pieces)
- Lavender
- Fennel Seeds
- Rosemary
- Horehound
- A few drops of lemongrass essential oil (optional)

Directions:

Blend all the ingredients together in a bowl or with a mortar and pestle and keep in a tightly sealed container.

VENUS

The only planet named for a female deity, Venus is named for the Roman goddess of love, beauty, and fertility, due to its brightness and its appearance in the morning sky. Deities from other cultures who are associated with Venus are Aphrodite, Astarte, Ishtar, Inanna, Isis, and Hathor.

In astrology, Venus represents beauty, love, culture, and the arts. In your natal chart, Venus shows you where you find pleasure in life, how you express love, and how you approach heart-based relationships. Venus represents worldly possessions and aesthetic taste, as well as what you value and what makes you feel good. Venus can show you what you love in life as well as your ability to attract partners and romance.

VENUS IN MAGIC

We work with the energy of Venus to help us succeed in matters of love and romance, attract pleasurable things into our lives, feel and look beautiful, create a sensual atmosphere, and feel love for ourselves and others.

If you want to align with the energy of Venus, consider going on a date, flirting with someone, writing a love letter (whether you send it or not), getting a makeover, adding a new piece of art to your home, visiting a museum, or watching a romantic movie.

VENUS CORRESPONDENCES

- **Magical Associations:** love, romance, charm, attraction, pleasure, beauty, harmony, sensuality, peacefulness, fertility

- **Plants, Herbs, Resins, and Essential Oils:** apple, cardamom, daisy, rose geranium, iris, lilac, magnolia, orchid, plumeria, rose, sweet pea, tansy, vanilla, violet, ylang-ylang

- **Crystals:** amazonite, aventurine, celestite, chrysocolla, emerald, green jasper, kunzite, jade, rhodochrosite, rhodonite, rose quartz

- **Foods of Venus for Nurturing and Sensual Delight:** acai berry, apples, avocado, blackberry, cherry, chocolate, peach, plum

- **Tarot card:** The Empress

- **Colors:** pink, emerald green, pastels

- **Day of the Week:** Friday

VENUS SPELL SACHET TO ATTRACT LOVE

This spell sachet is a charm you can carry with you to attract love into your life. It is recommendec you do this spell during a new moon in Taurus or Libra or on a Friday.

When choosing flowers to work with, you may want to research the Victorian language of flowers for inspiration.

You will need:

- Small velvet red bag
- A blend of dried flower petals, such as rose, daisy, geranium, iris, lavender, or orchid.
- A piece of rose quartz
- A piece of rhodonite
- Vanilla essential oil
- Rose essential oil (or rose absolute)
- A piece of paper and pink pen

Directions:

Take all the spell ingredients and blend them together in a bowl with your hands. As you work, envision the ingredients glowing pink and red.

Allow everything to warm up in your hands. Take your time with this, envisioning what you want this love to feel like. When you are satisfied with the blend, place the ingredients into the velvet bag.

Next, you will work with the pen and paper. Draw a large heart on the paper. Within the heart, write down the loving qualities you want to attract in your life. This can be as exact as "A romantic partner from Italy who is a Virgo" or more general, such as "self-love and patience with myself" or "life-long healthy friendships." Have fun writing these intentions and making them specific to your desires, and feel free to take up all the available space with your words.

When done, fold the paper and place it into the bag. Tie it up and carry it with you on dates or when meeting new people.

MARS

Mars is the Roman god of war, a fitting mascot for "the Red Planet." Mars was a protective god to the Romans, who valued their military prowess, but he was also a god of wisdom and strategy. Deities from other cultures who are associated with Mars are Ares, Durga, Macha, Odin, Set, Thor, and Anhur.

Mars in astrology represents instincts, work, energy, passion, and power. Mars in your natal chart shows you where you are most ambitious, where you are (or where you want to be) most powerful, what you are driven to do, and how you express anger. Mars also influences where you are assertive, independent, and determined. Mars can also show you how you experience raw sexual desire, what triggers you to anger, and the degree to which you are competitive with others.

MARS IN MAGIC

Mars has an assertive energy that helps us to feel empowered and energized. We work with Mars when we need a boost of willpower, need to muster up courage, or want to win in competitive situations.

If you want to align with the energy of Mars, consider visiting a volcano (or watching one safely from home), eating spicy food, wearing red, trying an intense workout like kickboxing, being safely and consensually sexual, reading the history of a war, or entering a competition.

MARS CORRESPONDENCES

- **Magical Associations:** action, ambition, assertiveness, channeling your rage and anger into healthier outlets, competition, courage, determination, empowerment, endurance, energy, excitement, protection, willpower

- **Plants, Herbs, Resins and Essential Oils:** allspice, basil, black pepper, bloodroot, cayenne, cinnamon, cumin, dragon's blood, galangal, garlic, ginger, nettle, paprika, woodruff

- **Crystals:** bloodstone, garnet, hematite, lodestone, ruby

- **Foods of Mars for Energy and Vitality:** coffee, ginger, horseradish, onion, pepper, spinach

- **Tarot card:** The Tower

- **Colors:** rust, red, magenta

- **Day of the Week:** Tuesday

MARS COFFEE SPELL FOR ENERGY

This invigorating chocolate, cinnamon, cayenne infused coffee will jump start your day and start you off feeling empowered.

You will need:

- Freshly brewed coffee
- ½ tsp. unsweetened cocoa powder
- Pinch or two of cinnamon
- Pinch of cayenne
- Milk, cream, and/or sweetener to taste

Directions:

Put the dry ingredients into the bottom of a large coffee cup. Slowly stir in the coffee, stirring in a clockwise direction. Say the following incantation as you stir:

"I have the courage of Mars and the energy to take meaningful actions today. May this coffee awaken my determination to stand proud and strong!"

Repeat this incantation three times, and stir in milk/cream, and/or sweetener to taste.

JUPITER

Jupiter is the largest planet in our solar system, which may be why both the Greeks and the Romans named it for their sky god (Zeus to the Greeks, and Jupiter to the Romans.) Jupiter is the god of sky and thunder, as well as the king of all the other Roman deities. While he could be a formidable presence, as symbolized by his thunderbolt, he was also considered a benevolent father figure who brought good fortune. Along with Zeus, deities from other cultures who are associated with Jupiter include Jove (another name for Jupiter), Amun, Hera, Justicia, Marduk, and Nut.

In astrology, Jupiter represents wealth, growth, luck, potential, and expansion. Jupiter's placement in your natal chart shows you where you are lucky in life, what you aspire to, and where you are most prosperous. Jupiter also influences how you express generosity, your capacity for optimism, and who or what you seek out for deeper truths. Tendencies to excessive indulgence and irresponsibility can also be illustrated by Jupiter in your chart.

JUPITER IN MAGIC

Jupiter energy can be worked with to bring us good luck. Jupiter energy is used for prosperity spells, financial wealth, good luck, abundance, generosity, and security.

If you want to align with the energy of Jupiter, consider creating a drawing or painting of Jupiter and its many wonderful colors, collecting coins, counting your blessings, "paying it forward," carrying a good luck charm, donating to a good cause, watching a thunderstorm, raising money for those in need, or doing charity work.

JUPITER CORRESPONDENCES

- **Magical Associations:** good luck, hope, influence, money, prosperity, optimistic outcomes, wealth, generosity

- **Plants, Herbs, Resins and Essential Oils:** bay leaves, cinquefoil, clove, garden sage, honeysuckle, hyssop, mace, nutmeg, oakmoss, star anise, tonka bean, frankincense

- **Crystals:** ametrine, lepidolite, tiger's eye, yellow sapphire, yellow topaz

- **Foods of Jupiter for Increased Health and Wellness:** alfalfa, broccoli, Brussels sprouts, millet, olives, pumpkins, squash walnut

- **Tarot card:** The Wheel of Fortune

- **Colors:** purple, indigo

- **Day of the Week:** Thursday

JUPITER JAR SPELL FOR PROSPERITY

This jar is meant to honor the beautiful bands of Jupiter by building layers of ingredients that will help bring money into your life.

It is recommended that you find a jar on the smaller side, even a clear glass vial or a half-ounce spice jar, so you do not need to fill it with an excess or expensive number of items.

You will need:

- A purple or indigo spell candle
- Honey
- Coins
- Tiger's eye crystal chips
- Frankincense resin
- Cloves
- Dried and crushed oak and/or bay leaves
- Gold glitter
- Small piece of paper and green pen

Directions:

Light the spell candle. Then take the pen and write the words "Fortune, Good Luck, Wealth and Prosperity from Jupiter" on the paper.

Cover the rest of the space on the paper with dollar signs. If you want to be extra creative with this step, print out a blank check image and write a check to yourself for as large of a sum as you would like. Fold this paper into a small piece and place it into the bottom of the jar.

You are now going to have fun layering the ingredients, and separating each ingredient layer with a thin layer of honey. I recommend starting with the heaviest ingredients, using the order of the list above as a recommended guide. Feel free to add, omit, or modify what you include in the jar to make it uniquely yours.

Hold the jar in your hands and envision the energies of Jupiter infusing the ingredients and expanding the prosperity in your life. Set it in front of the spell candle and allow the candle to burn out on its own. Keep this jar near where you work, on your altar, or on your hearth.

SATURN

Saturn was the outermost planet visible to the naked eye, and therefore the last of the planets known to ancient astronomers. Its lengthy orbit inspired the ancient Greeks to name the ringed planet for Kronos, the god of time. The Romans named it for their equivalent god, Saturn, a god of time and restrictions. His festival, Saturnalia, was a big celebration in ancient Rome, when the normal social and moral codes were dropped in favor of wild celebrations each December. In addition to Kronos, deities from other cultures who are associated with Saturn include Ganesh, Amun, Durga, Ceres, Demeter, and Geb.

Saturn in astrology represents responsibilities, karma, limitations, obstacles, and delays. Saturn's placement in your chart shows you where you need more organization and discipline in your life, how you handle responsibilities, and where you feel limited or insecure. Saturn's restrictive energy can be thought of as a counter to the expansiveness of Jupiter, creating the necessary containers for what we want to manifest. Saturn may offer difficult lessons, but they're opportunities to examine where you need to create boundaries in your life in order to thrive.

SATURN IN MAGIC

Saturn energy can be a little volatile, but even so, it's beneficial in purification, banishment, and cleaning magic. If you feel you have obstacles in your way, consider working with Saturn to assist in the removal of what does not benefit you.

If you want to align with Saturn energy, consider wearing a watch, using an hourglass to time yourself as you work through chores, using smoke from herbs or incense to purify your home, building a protection spell bottle, making a to-do list, prioritizing responsibilities, and asking for help from your support system.

SATURN CORRESPONDENCES

- **Magical Associations:** banishment, boundaries, closure, endurance, karma, patience, purification, strength through overcoming obstacles

- **Plants, Herbs, Resins and Essential Oils:** cannabis, chaga, comfrey, cypress, garlic, hyssop, nettle, patchouli, Solomon's seal, spikenard, valerian root

- **Essential Oils:** cypress, patchouli

- **Crystals:** hematite, obsidian, tourmaline, onyx

- **Foods of Saturn for Instilling Healthy Habits:** activated charcoal, beets, black beans, blackcurrant, eggplant, figs, garlic, pomegranate

- **Tarot card:** The World

- **Colors:** brown, dark green
- **Day of the Week:** Saturday

SATURN PROTECTION RING

This simple spell calls on the protective energies of Saturn and the symbolism of this planet's infamous rings. Hematite rings are said to absorb negativity and protect the wearer from negative energy and harm. They are affordable and easy to find in metaphysical shops. You will need just one hematite ring for this spell, which is best performed on a Saturday.

Cleanse your hematite ring of any unwanted energies by running it through purifying smoke or leaving it in direct sunlight for a few hours. When you're ready to charge it for use, hold the ring in your hand and say the following incantation:

"Ring of Saturn, protect me from negative energy and harm!"

Say this as many times as you would like to. When you feel the ring is sufficiently charged, put it on.

Note: Hematite is a brittle stone that can break more easily than other crystals used in jewelry. This property works in our favor, however, as it's said that a hematite ring will break when it has absorbed all the negativity it can. If and when this happens, take the broken ring and bury it. Replace with a new one if you would like to, and repeat this spell again.

URANUS

While it's believed that ancient astrologers may have been aware of Uranus, it was not determined to be a planet until 1781, and its name didn't become officially recognized until 1850. The only planet named for a Greek god, Uranus was discovered during the American Revolution and a few years before the French Revolution.

This is interesting timing, given that the main myth Uranus is known for ends with his demise at the hands of his son Kronos, as revenge for Uranus' mistreatment of his children. Uranus was the Greeks' primordial god of the sky, who existed before Zeus. Deities from other cultures who are associated with Uranus are Caelus and Nut.

In astrology, Uranus represents eccentricity, technology and innovation, revolution, enlightenment, and originality. In your natal chart, Uranus influences how you break from tradition and what motivates you to rock the boat. Uranus can reveal what makes you a magical, one-of-a-kind being, but it can also show where you feel misunderstood or where you may be unnecessarily rebellious. Think of Uranus as revealing your unique human experience.

URANUS IN MAGIC

Uranus energy is electric, exciting, transformative, and revolutionary. We harness Uranus' energy in magic to bring about transformation, freedom from restrictions, and significant change. You can also find your calling, your unique community, and your ties to the occult through working with Uranus energy.

If you wish to align with Uranus energy, consider learning about astral travel, reading science fiction, studying the occult, finding a cause to become active in, making new friends, embracing your unique quirks, getting a massage to relieve tension, or getting a picture of your aura taken.

URANUS CORRESPONDENCES

- **Magical Associations:** alchemy, astral travel, change, community, freedom, independence, innovation, inspiration, originality, release, revolution, uniqueness

- **Plants, Herbs, Resins and Essential Oils:** blue chamomile, coffee, eucalyptus, ginkgo, kava kava, lime, neroli, skullcap, star anise

- **Crystals:** amazonite, angelite, azurite, labradorite, moldavite, nummite, sodalite

- **Foods of Uranus:** sustainable, local, and/or organic food, cross-cultural fusion dishes

- **Tarot card:** the Fool

- **Colors:** teal, sky blue, blue

URANUS CRYSTAL GRID TO HELP AWAKEN YOUR UNIQUE MAGIC

Crystal grids are specific patterns of crystals and mineral stones that can be built in order to work directly with subtle energies. A grid can amplify positive energy, protect a space from negative energy, or direct energy toward a magical goal. Build this crystal grid when you are looking to find new paths to explore in your life, conjure up inspiration, and help you tap into your unique brand of magic. If possible, this grid is wonderful to create outdoors under a clear night sky.

For this grid, you will need the following crystals placed out as the graph shows:

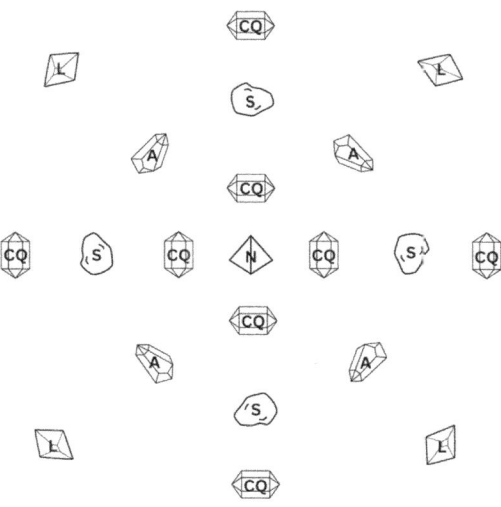

- **N:** Nummite is known as the "Sorcerer's Stone" and is used for meditation, self-love, breaking through confusion, and seeing who you are at your spiritual core.

- **CQ:** Crystal Quartz to awaken the crystal grid's energy and bring clarity and insight into the space.

- **S:** Sodalite to stimulate intuition, promote peace and calm, and assist with seeing honest truths about yourself.

- **A:** Amazonite to conjure hopefulness, heal heartache from past disappointments, and inspire visions for a new, better future.

- **L:** Labradorite to stimulate psychic abilities and clairvoyant visions, promote innovative thinking, and honor the magic of imagination.

You can leave the grid in place for as long as you feel it is benefiting you.

To get the maximum benefit, spend time in meditation with the grid each day. If you're creating a large grid, sit in the center to meditate while holding your piece of nummite. If it is a smaller grid, keep the nummite in the center. When you open the grid, carry the nummite with you as an amulet.

NEPTUNE

Neptune was discovered in 1846, and was named after the Roman god of the sea because of its vibrant ultramarine blue color. Although the god Neptune was not known for having a pleasant temperament, his link to the element of water is significant—the planet was discovered during the height of the Spiritualism and Transcendentalism movements, which were concerned with metaphysical beliefs and practices. Deities from other cultures who are associated with Neptune are Poseidon, Enki, and Khnum.

In astrology, Neptune represents spirituality, mysticism, and idealism. Neptune's placement in your chart reveals how you can tap into psychic abilities to transcend this reality and go into higher realms of knowing. It influences what you are drawn to spiritually, and what inspires you to optimism and idealism. However, Neptune also represents illusions, deception, and addictions, so it can also reveal what you want to escape from in your life, or where you may even deceive yourself and others. Its lessons can help you to examine your authentic self more closely. Think of Neptune as illuminating your path to spiritual ascension.

NEPTUNE IN MAGIC

Neptune energy is all about poetry, art, mysticism, spirituality, and dreams. We can use Neptune energy in magic to conjure deep spiritual awareness, mystical visions, vivid dreams, and esoteric self-expression.

If you are looking to connect with Neptune energy, visit the ocean, work with marine life conservation efforts, try snorkeling, attend a watercolor painting workshop, scry in a reflective body of water, go to a therapy session, practice any form of divination, or read about the legends of Atlantis.

NEPTUNE CORRESPONDENCES

- **Magical Associations:** clairvoyance, dreamy creativity, imagination, intuition, mystical visions, Otherworldly visions, psychic awareness, spirituality, spiritual awakening, water magic

- **Plants, Herbs, Resins and Essential Oils for Neptune:** bladderwrack, blue lotus, butterfly pea flower, hemp, marshmallow root, poppy, reed, sea buckthorn, waterlily, wisteria

- **Crystals connected to Neptune:** aquamarine, angelite, labradorite, lapis lazuli, lepidolite

- **Foods of Neptune for Tranquil and Balanced Energy:** blueberry, green tea, seafood, seaweed, vegetable juice, watermelon

- **Tarot card:** The Hanged Man
- **Colors:** blue, sea green, indigo

MYSTICAL NEPTUNE WATERCOLOR DIVINATION

For this spell, which was inspired by astrologer Maighdlin Kelly, you will need a set of watercolors, a paintbrush, and watercolor or other durable paper. If you are artistically inclined, you may find that a paintbrush feels much like a magical wand, awakening magic and mystical talents as you move it across the canvas.

First, brush a light coating of water on the paper. Then take whichever watercolor paints you are called to use and dab some on the page with your brush. You will find that the paint spreads across the page, taking different shapes or forms in whichever direction the water influences the paint to move. (If you want to try something extra mystical, close your eyes before you begin!) Repeat this process until most or all of the page is covered.

When you feel finished painting, gently pick up the page and lightly tilt it back and forth, or side to side—whichever direction calls to you. Then place the paper down on the table and begin to examine it. What colors stand out to you and what do those colors represent to you? Do you see any symbols or images appear in the painting? Are there any letters or words? As you examine the painting, what divinatory interpretations might you make about what you are seeing?

PLUTO

Pluto is named for the Roman god of the Underworld, presiding over the kingdom of the dead. Although it is now technically classified as a dwarf planet, Pluto is still considered a planet in astrology, as it has been included as such for nearly a century. Whether the astronomers at that time knew it or not, the name Pluto was a perfect fit for the energies of this planet, which are associated with sweeping transformation and the unseen.

The existence of Pluto was first theorized in 1905, but it remained hidden from view until it was discovered in 1930—a pivotal time in modern history between two world wars, and at the beginning of the Great Depression. Deities from other cultures who are associated with Pluto are Hades, Hecate, Kali, the Morrigan, Ereshkigal, and Osiris.

Pluto in astrology represents transformation, rebirth, the subconscious, and things hidden below the surface. In your natal chart, Pluto shows you where you need to break old patterns, what issues need to be resolved in your life, and what complicated matters or upheavals can be transformed into lessons for growth. Pluto's movements from one sign to another can reveal complex issues that have been hidden from the world. Think of Pluto as revealing the nature of transformation throughout the course of this life.

PLUTO IN MAGIC

Pluto energy is all about rebirth, renewal, and new beginnings. We work with Pluto energy in magic when we are ready for new beginnings, need assistance working through grief, are encountering our shadow self, or dealing with difficult times. This isn't always the easiest magic to work with, but it can help you move into phases that will bring in beneficial opportunities.

If you want to align with Pluto energy, go to a therapy session, read the Egyptian Book of the Dead, watch some true crime mysteries, keep an altar to honor your ancestors, or visit a graveyard.

PLUTO CORRESPONDENCES

- **Magical Associations:** moving through difficult phases, karma, rebirth, redemption, relinquishing control, shadow work, spirit quests, transformation, transitions

- **Plants, Herbs, Resins and Essential Oils:** cypress, pine, pomegranate

- **Crystals:** black tourmaline, hypersthene, jet, tourmalated quartz

- **Tarot card:** Judgment

- **Colors:** black, maroon, steel gray

PLUTO GENERATIONAL STUDY

Because Pluto is so far away from Earth, it can remain in one sign from 12 to 23 years. This makes Pluto a marker for generational energy and characteristics.

The following lists Pluto's five most recent transits and the names of the generations corresponding with these transits. Using this information, you can delve into a study of generational differences. Which Pluto Generation are you a part of? How does the sign of your natal Pluto differ from that of your parents, grandparents, and/or children?

Compare the characteristics of these generations with the zodiac descriptions in Chapter 3. How do these comparisons help you deepen your understanding of zodiac and planetary energies?

- Pluto was in Leo from 1939 to 1958, loosely tying in with the Silent Generation and Baby Boomers.

- Pluto was in Virgo from 1956 to 1971, loosely tying in with younger Boomers and older members of Generation X.

- Pluto was in Libra from 1971 to 1983, loosely tying in with younger Gen Xers and older Millennials.

- Pluto was in Scorpio from 1983 to 1995, loosely tying in with the majority of Millennials.

- Pluto was in Sagittarius from 1996 to 2009, loosely tying in with Generation Z.

OTHER CELESTIAL BODIES

Today's astrologers do not just work with the luminaries and the planets in our solar system. There are other, smaller celestial bodies, such as dwarf planets and asteroids, that can influence us astrologically, and many witches believe their energies can be used in magic as well.

Most of these bodies were discovered in the 19th and 20th centuries, while others have come into our awareness in the new millennium. They are found either within the asteroid belt between Mars and Jupiter, or the more recently discovered Kuiper Belt, in the outer reaches of the solar system. Note that this is not an exhaustive list, and that astrologers are still exploring the energies of these new discoveries.

Body	Classification	Location	Named For	Magical Associations
Chiron	Planetoid	Between Saturn and Uranus	Greek Centaur, known as the "Wounded Healer"	Emotional and spiritual healing, wisdom, helping others heal

Body	Classification	Location	Named For	Magical Associations
Juno	Asteroid	Between Mars and Jupiter	Roman goddess of marriage	Relationships (with people and money/finances)
Ceres	Dwarf Planet	Between Mars and Jupiter	Roman Earth goddess	Nurturing, self-care, women's mysteries, menstrual cycles, protection
Hygeia	Asteroid	Between Mars and Jupiter	Personification of cleanliness and well-being. Daughter of Asclepius, Greek god of medicine.	Healthy habits, well-being, hygiene, establishing and maintaining health
Eris	Dwarf Planet	Kuiper Belt	Greek goddess of revenge, discord, and rivalry.	Chaos magic, handling resentment, indignation, speaking up
Vesta	Asteroid	Between Mars and Jupiter	Roman goddess of the hearth fire	Sacred sexuality, intimacy, passion, spirituality, soul callings
Makemake	Dwarf Planet	Kuiper Belt	Polynesian creator god of Easter Island	Abundance, fertility, working with nature, healing the Earth, manifesting dreams

Body	Classification	Location	Named For	Magical Associations
Varuna	Asteroid	Kuiper Belt	Hindu creation god of the sky, rain, ocean, law, and the Underworld	Law and order, legal matters, fame, praise, water magic
Sedna	Dwarf Planet	Beyond Kuiper Belt	Inuit goddess of the sea, hopes, dreams, and false promises	Dealing with feelings of isolation or disconnectedness from others

PLANETARY DIVINATION SPREAD

Use this divination spread with tarot cards, oracle cards, or any other divination tools you use. Each placement here is meant to connect you with the energies and advice of the astrological planets.

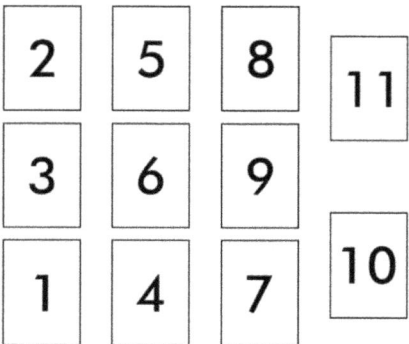

- **Card One represents EARTH.** Here you will see current events impacting you and how you are feeling presently.
- **Card Two represents the SUN.** Here you will see where you have potential to grow.

- **Card Three represents the MOON.** Here you will see emotions that you need to focus on, explore, heal, and/or express.
- **Card Four represents MERCURY.** Here you will see something you need to study, research, and learn about.
- **Card Five represents VENUS.** Here you will see important relationships or partnerships that can add value and pleasure to your life.
- **Card Six represents MARS.** Here you will see where you need to be determined and work hard in your life.
- **Card Seven represents JUPITER.** Here you will see how you can bring good luck, fortune, and prosperity into your life.
- **Card Eight represents SATURN.** Here you will examine obstacles you must face, lessons you can learn from, and habits and behavior patterns to release.
- **Card Nine represents URANUS.** Look here for suggestions to view your life from a fresh perspective. These are innovative new ideas to try out.
- **Card Ten represents NEPTUNE.** Here you will find guidance for exploring your magical powers, tapping into spirituality more deeply, and awakening your psychic abilities.
- **Card Eleven represents PLUTO.** Here you will see what evolutions and transformations you are meant to journey through in the near future.

Chapter Three: OUR ENCHANTED ZODIAC: ENERGY, MOODS, AND MAGIC OF EACH SIGN

The exact origins of the zodiac are difficult to determine, as it is found in various forms across ancient cultures and evolved over time into the form we understand today. To the best of our knowledge, the zodiac first appeared in Mesopotamia (later, Babylonia) during the 1st millennium BCE. Eventually, it was adapted by the ancient Greeks, and later, the Romans. The English word "zodiac" is originally Greek for "cycle (or circle) of animals," as most of the signs are associated with animals or animal-like figures from ancient myths.

The typical start and end dates of each zodiac sign are as follows. Note that these dates can change slightly from one year to the next, depending on the date of the Spring

Equinox, which is the beginning of the astrological year and can vary slightly with the calendar year. If your birthday falls on or close to one of the dates listed here, go with the sign the sun was in on your actual birth date.

- **Aries:** March 21 to April 19
- **Taurus:** April 20 to May 20
- **Gemini:** May 21 to June 20
- **Cancer:** June 21 to July 22
- **Leo:** July 23 to August 22
- **Virgo:** August 23 to September 22
- **Libra:** September 23 to October 22
- **Scorpio:** October 23 to November 21
- **Sagittarius:** November 22 to December 21
- **Capricorn:** December 22 to January 19
- **Aquarius:** January 20 to February 18
- **Pisces:** February 19 to March 20

In this chapter we are going to explore the mythology, astrological energies, character traits, and magical qualities and correspondences of each of the zodiac signs. We will also look at the three significant placements in our personal natal charts and how these signs can influence our personality traits.

The goal of this chapter is to deepen your understanding of who you are based on your Sun, Moon, and Rising signs, or the "Big Three." However, the energies of the signs you don't have in your chart are still relevant, as they affect the world at large, and correspond with particular magical intentions, as you will see in the descriptions below.

THE BIG THREE

In *You Were Born for This,* author Chani Nicholas reflects on the profound, even divine value of the natal chart: "Your birth chart is a snapshot of the sky the moment you took your first breath. It marks your arrival here on earth; a celestial blueprint, if you will, that holds the keys to living a life of purpose." We look at the "Big Three" as opposed to just the Sun sign because it gives us a more detailed and well-rounded examination of your personality, which is as complex as astrology itself.

Within the overall field of astrology, there is a general consensus that the "Big Three" are the most significant placements in your chart to understand, but not all astrologers view them in the exact same way. One branch of the field, known as esoteric astrology, differs from what we often call "popular" astrology in that it views the Big Three in the context of reincarnation, and the soul lessons we're here to learn in this lifetime.

Not all astrologers believe in reincarnation, and neither do all witches, but many in both groups do. Even leaving aside the concept of past lives, many believe that we choose certain experiences and aspects of our lives before we're born, and choose our time and place of birth in order to embody the astrological energies that will shape our human nature, the lessons we're here to learn, and the purposes we're here to serve.

In other words, your natal chart is not random, but part of the inherent magic of your unique existence. This belief is not required in order to understand the information presented here, but it's worth considering as you learn more about your natal chart and its implications for your life.

Your Sun sign shows you where the sun was when you were born. This is a top-level glimpse into your core personality and your conscious identity. In esoteric astrology, the Sun represents qualities you intended to develop and express in this incarnation, and its placement in your natal chart indicates something about your overall focus in this current lifetime. Your Sun sign influences your motivations and your egoic self, and can also indicate natural talents.

If you don't have other planets beyond the Sun in this sign, or if your Moon or Rising signs are at odds with your Sun energetically, you may not actually feel very identified with your Sun sign. This doesn't mean that you don't possess the qualities of this sign, but that other aspects of your chart are more dominant for you. It's often noted that people start identifying more with their Sun sign as they get older, as it's through life experience that we truly get to know who we are at our core.

Your Moon sign reveals your inner world. The Moon represents the subconscious, our inner desires, our emotional self, and what we keep hidden from all but those closest to us. In esoteric astrology, the Moon's placement in your chart indicates what you have brought with you from past incarnations into this lifetime.

Past-life experiences, both positive and negative, still influence us on a subconscious level, acting as "psychic imprints" on our emotional tendencies, behavioral patterns, and natural instincts. Your Moon sign helps identify where you are the most comfortable, how you behave in private, how you express your feelings, and how you can experience and navigate your emotions in healthy and beneficial ways.

Your Rising sign is the sign that was rising over the eastern horizon at the moment of your birth. Also known as your Ascendent, the Rising sign reflects how you appear to the world around you, what you present to the world, and how you interact with others.

As mentioned in the Introduction, if the Sun sign represents an actor, the Rising sign represents the mask the actor wears. Depending on their placements, this "mask" may be similar to the energy of your Sun sign, or quite different. For example, if your Sun and Rising are the same sign, there's little difference between your core self and the image you present to the world. But if the energies of your Rising sign are very different from your Sun sign, your core self may not be readily apparent to others at all.

Esoteric astrologers believe that the Rising sign indicates your soul's purpose, as every other planet and placement in your natal chart is filtered through the energies of your Rising sign. Some also believe that in order to fully achieve our soul's purpose in this life, the negative or challenging qualities of our Sun sign must be tamed or balanced so that the positive qualities of the Rising sign can fully flourish.

The following descriptions reveal traits of each zodiac sign as they apply to Sun, Moon, and Rising placements in your chart. You'll also find magical ideas, spiritual prompts, and activity suggestions for each sign to help you make the most of the energies of your Big Three placements. Explore the possibilities presented here in order to feel more comfortable and confident in your own skin, find inner peace, and enjoy the world around you.

ARIES

- **Aries Season:** March 21 to April 19. Aries begins on the Spring Equinox (Ostara) in the Northern Hemisphere, and on the Autumn Equinox (Mabon) in the Southern Hemisphere.
- **Symbol:** the Ram
- **Ruling planet:** Mars
- **Element:** fire
- **Colors:** red, scarlet, pink
- **Keywords:** active, ambitious, confidence, driven, passionate
- **Magical correspondences:** beginnings, confidence, fire magic, initiation, lust, passion, optimism, strength, taking action
- **Plants, herbs, resins, and essential oils:** allspice, angelica, cayenne, cedar, cinnamon, cloves, copal resin, dragon's blood, frankincense, ginger, galangal, garlic, musk, poppy
- **Crystals:** bloodstone, carnelian, diamond, fire opal, garnet, hematite, steel, red jasper, ruby
- **Tarot Card:** the Emperor

CONJURING ARIES ENERGY

Aries is named for Ares, the Greek god of war. However, its energies are also associated with Mars, the Roman god of war, which is also Aries' ruling planet. To the Greeks, Ares was an unpredictable and destructive god, and therefore was not particularly revered. Mars, while also fierce and hot-tempered, was a beloved father god to the Romans, and his warrior energy was used to protect the stability of Rome. The symbol of Aries, the golden ram, comes from Greek mythology and represents strength, courage, and great power.

Aries are known to be go-getters: they are active, eager, and assertive. We can work with Aries energy when we must begin new projects. As the first sign in the zodiac, Aries awakens the Zodiac Year with a "Big Bang" energy, entering the cosmic stage with passion, fierceness, and eagerness. Magical amulets to conjure the energy of Aries include drinking horns, swords, and/or athames.

ARIES SUN SIGN

Those who have an Aries Sun are animated, confident, and courageous. They can be good at starting new projects, but can get bored with those projects quickly. Aries Sun can handle stressful situations and are willing to take risks.

If your Sun sign is Aries, remember to slow down and process your heated feelings rather than reacting in an aggressive way. Aries can be influenced by salamander energy, the magical beings said to represent the element of fire and help bring good luck.

Magic to highlight Aries Sun:

- Use athames or wands in your magical rituals
- Wear a spicy fragrance that has cinnamon or ginger in it
- Try a high-level cardio activity like running or kickboxing

ARIES MOON SIGN

Those with Moon in Aries can be direct, intense, and bold. They love to be surrounded by bright colors. They feel comfort in exciting situations and are optimistic in the face of challenges, having an inner confidence that helps them overcome obstacles.

Magic to balance Moon in Aries:

- Use seven-day candles to burn for spells
- Take some time in a sauna
- Drink ginger tea
- Decorate your home with bright, bold colors

ARIES RISING SIGN

Aries Rising signs appear as competitive, independent, and born leaders. They are highly energetic people who love to be on the winning team. They are very straightforward and cut to the point to get quick results.

Magic to celebrate your Aries Rising:

- Work with fire magic
- Try pyromancy, which is divination with fire
- Help others with planning and starting high energy projects

TAURUS

- **Taurus Season:** April 20 to May 20. In the Wheel of the Year, the Taurus season hosts Beltane in the Northern Hemisphere and Samhain in the Southern Hemisphere.
- **Symbol:** the Bull
- **Ruling planet:** Venus
- **Element:** earth
- **Colors:** green, pink
- **Keywords:** abundant, comfortable, grounded, sensual, stable
- **Magical correspondences:** abundance, art, beauty, comfort, creativity, earth magic, fertility, growth, love, loving homestead, luxury, manifestation, patience, wealth
- **Plants, herbs, resins, and essential oils:** daisy, dandelion, foxglove, geranium, heather, honeysuckle, lilac, magnolia, musk, patchouli, plumeria, raspberry, rose, tonka bean, vanilla, violet
- **Crystals:** azurite, chrysocolla, emerald, jade, kunzite, malachite, moss agate, peridot, rhodonite, rose quartz
- **Tarot card:** the Hierophant

CONJURING TAURUS ENERGY

Taurus is associated with the Greek god Zeus, who took the form of a beautiful white bull in order to convince the goddess Europa to go away with him and become his lover. The energies of this sign combine the earthy stubbornness of the bull with the sensual beauty and romance of Venus, its ruling planet.

Tauruses are known to be loyal, artistic, sensual, grounded, stubborn, and possessive. They love to enjoy the pleasures of life, taking their time to soak up the beauty their surroundings offer them. We can work with Taurus energy when we are looking to bring abundance and sensual pleasure into our lives. Magical amulets to conjure the energy of Taurus include horns, a torc, and/or spring flowers.

TAURUS SUN SIGN

Those who have Taurus Sun are loyal, grounded, comforting, and decadent. Tauruses are resourceful, slow moving, and slow to accept change. They can be influenced by Gaia energy, vibing well with Mother Earth worship. They love art and love to be surrounded by beautiful things. If your Sun sign is Taurus, try to remember to push out of your comfort zone every now than then.

Magic to highlight Taurus Sun:

- Decorate your altar with spring flowers
- Wear a floral fragrance like rose or ylang-ylang

- Enjoy a walk in a rose garden or a summer picnic in the park

TAURUS MOON SIGN

Those with Moon in Taurus can be nurturing, patient, and sensual. They have an attractive and loving energy that draws people to them very naturally. They love to be surrounded by luxurious things, like unique art and crystals.

Magic to balance Moon in Taurus:

- Fill your home with pretty house plants and crystals for prosperity
- Buy yourself, or someone you adore, a bouquet of flowers
- Spend quality time with a loyal friend

TAURUS RISING SIGN

Taurus Rising signs appear loyal, supportive, and generous. They love all things beautiful, can be very artistic looking, and want to ensure the comfort of all of those around them. They are happy and friendly, so others gravitate to the warmth they radiate.

Magic to celebrate your Taurus Rising:

- Wear malachite or emerald jewelry
- Practice garden magic by planting and nurturing magical herbs and flowers
- Share herbs and holistic concoctions with your close friends

GEMINI

- **Gemini Season:** May 21 to June 20
- **Symbol:** the Twins
- **Ruling planet:** Mercury
- **Element:** air
- **Colors:** white, yellow
- **Keywords:** clear-cut, intelligent, thoughtful, witty, wise
- **Magical correspondences:** air magic, balance, clarification, entertainment, intelligence, knowledge, speaking, social abilities, travel, writing, variety, wit
- **Plants, herbs, resins, and essential oils:** almond, anise, bergamot, citron, daisy, dill, eyebright, fennel, hazel, horehound, iris, lavender, lily of the valley, lemongrass, marjoram, peppermint, vervain, wormwood, yarrow
- **Crystals:** agate, alexandrite, apophyllite, citrine, chrysocolla, crystal quartz, howlite, moonstone, pearl, rutilated quartz
- **Tarot card:** the Lovers

CONJURING GEMINI ENERGY

Gemini is a constellation associated with the twin figures Castor and Pollux, who accomplished many heroic feats and were considered the patron gods of horses by the Romans. The mythology of the twins gives Gemini its associations with duality and partnership, while its ruling planet, Mercury, embodies its airy, communicative energies.

Geminis are known for their cleverness, adaptability, and love of talking. They are known as being incredibly intelligent and quick to respond to questions with eloquent answers. We can work with Gemini energy to assist with communication, public speaking, teaching, learning, and writing. Magical amulets and objects to conjure Gemini energy include silver coins, scrying mirrors and censers for burning incense.

GEMINI SUN SIGN

Those who have Gemini Sun are energetic and agile, and have a gift for communication. They are excellent teachers and writers, but must learn how to focus their thoughts. Geminis are creative, adaptable, and love mental stimulation, making them popular with a diverse group of friends. They can be influenced by trickster energy, getting easily distracted and being prone to gossip and talking in circles or riddles.

If your Sun sign is Gemini, ensure that you take a break from the social world if you are feeling anxious or agitated.

Magic to highlight Gemini Sun:

- Take the time to create and use a Book of Shadows
- Work with spirit boards or try automatic writing
- Wear bright fragrances like lemongrass or lily of the valley

GEMINI MOON SIGN

Those with Moon in Gemini love to hold space with smart and creative people. They love to be surrounded by books and like to keep their windows open. They feel best when they can discuss what is on their mind, sharing their thoughts openly with those they care about. If your Moon sign is Gemini, you love change and need to be mindful of feeling scattered or worried.

Magic to balance Moon in Gemini:

- Repeat mantras and incantations to assist with magic
- Use lavender aromatherapy at the end of the day to unwind and relax
- Practice grounding by standing, walking, or sitting with your bare feet on the ground

GEMINI RISING SIGN

Gemini Rising signs appear as social, witty multitaskers. They are excellent storytellers, but also can clearly point out everything that is going on around them. They have a tendency to be busybodies with smart and quick responses to everything. If your Rising sign is Gemini, you are easy to talk to and fun to bounce ideas off of.

Magic to celebrate your Gemini Rising:

- Research a magical topic and share the information you found with your friends
- Teach a magical workshop
- Host a witchy podcast

CANCER

- **Cancer Season:** June 21 to July 22. Cancer begins on the Summer Solstice (Litha) in the Northern Hemisphere, and on the Winter Solstice (Yule) in the Southern Hemisphere.
- **Symbol:** the Crab
- **Ruling planet:** Moon
- **Element:** water
- **Colors:** light blue, sea green, silver, white
- **Keywords:** caring, intuitive, moody, nurturing, sensitive
- **Magical correspondences:** balancing moods, emotional calmness, empathy, family, homestead, introspection, intuition, lunar magic, peacefulness, psychic awareness
- **Plants, herbs, resins, and essential oils:** aloe, amber, camphor, catnip, coconut, gardenia, jasmine, lemon, lemon balm, lotus, milkweed, moonwort, mugwort, myrrh, sandalwood, seaweed, tuberose, water lily, willow
- **Crystals:** blue calcite, jasper, moonstone, opal, pearl, rose quartz, ruby, sapphire, sea salt, selenite
- **Tarot card:** the Chariot

CONJURING CANCER ENERGY

Cancer is named for the giant crab of Greek mythology who was created by Hera in order to assist the sea monster Hydra in a battle against Heracles. Hera was the goddess of women, marriage, family, and childbirth, and was revered as the Queen of Olympus. This sign's feminine, watery energies are further enhanced by its ruling planet, the Moon.

Cancers are known to be nurturing, vulnerable, moody, and sensitive. They are known for liking to stay close to home, perhaps much like a crab hiding in his shell. Cancer energy can be used for psychic work, divination, domestic blessings, and balancing moods. Magical amulets and objects to conjure Cancer energy include shells, chalices, and crab claws.

CANCER SUN SIGN

Those who have Cancer Sun are nurturing, empathic, and moody. It's valuable for Cancer Suns to psychically shield themselves from the feelings, opinions, and emotions of others.

If your Sun is in Cancer, it's crucial to also be dedicated to uplifting your self-esteem. Cancers can be influenced by mermaid energy, hidden in their cavernous dwellings deep within the ocean of their emotions.

Magic to highlight Cancer Sun:

- Perform magic at the ocean
- Wear a soothing fragrance like coconut or vanilla

- Keep a dream journal

CANCER MOON SIGN

Those with Moon in Cancer are sensitive and love a gentle, soft life. They are very empathic, able to pick up on the energy around them very easily. If your Moon sign is in Cancer, it is important for you to not get lost in romanticized, sentimental memories. Instead, look to what can keep your emotions joyously regulated in the present moment.

Magic to balance Moon in Cancer:

- Have a relaxing Epsom salt bath
- Drink chamomile tea
- Do magic to purify the energy of your home regularly

CANCER RISING SIGN

Cancer Rising signs are gentle caregivers who can be very affectionate. Because of their sensitive nature, they can be empathic but also moody. They can come off as shy or quiet, but are more open and vulnerable if they feel safe and comfortable with their surroundings.

Magic to celebrate your Cancer Rising:

- Celebrate lunar magic with close friends and family
- Practice psychometry by touching objects or buildings and seeing if you pick up on any psychic premonitions
- Wear or carry moonstone, selenite, aquamarine, labradorite, or rainbow jasper

LEO

- **Leo Season:** July 23 to August 22. In the Wheel of the Year, the Leo season hosts Lughnasadh in the Northern Hemisphere and Imbolc in the Southern Hemisphere.
- **Symbol:** the Lion
- **Ruling planet:** Sun
- **Element:** fire
- **Colors:** orange, gold
- **Keywords:** bold, courageous, creative, determined, friendly
- **Magical correspondences:** ambition, charisma, courage, confidence, empowerment, fire magic, friendship, happiness, loyalty, optimism, passion, sun magic, willpower
- **Plants, herbs, resins, and essential oils:** amber, angelica, carnation, cinnamon, cloves, copal, firebush, frankincense, goldenseal, heliotrope, marigold, nutmeg, orange, passionflower, saffron, St. John's Wort, sunflower
- **Crystals:** amber, garnet, morganite, peridot, pyrite, ruby, tiger's eye, topaz
- **Tarot card:** Strength

CONJURING LEO ENERGY

The word Leo is derived from both Latin and Greek words for "lion." The myth associated with this sign is the defeat by Heracles of the Nemian lion, a deadly beast whose thick pelt was impenetrable to weaponry. This sign's energies align with both the symbolism of the lion (strength and sovereignty) as well as the characteristics of Heracles (passion, emotion, and courage). These qualities are further emphasized by the Sun, Leo's ruling planet.

Leos are known to be "larger than life" personalities. Leos can be dramatic, idealistic, charismatic, and magnetic. They are known for being very charitable, generous, and loyal to those they love. Leo energy can be used to bring fun into your life. Magical amulets and objects used to conjure Leo energy include citrine pendants, wands, and candles.

LEO SUN SIGN

Those who have Leo Sun are strong-willed, honest, creative, and theatrical. They are known to be attention-seeking and have the charm to receive what they desire. They must be mindful not to become too self-centered or vain. Leos can be influenced by the solar energy of the Sphinx, boldly presiding over an awe-inspired kingdom of magic and lore.

Magic to highlight Leo Sun:

- Perform theatrical or ceremonial magic
- Sit on a patio with friends for Sunday brunch

- Wear a spicy and sunny fragrance like frankincense or amber

LEO MOON SIGN

Those with Moon in Leo find laughter to be healing. They like to have a playful and fun energy around them to keep their spirits high, and feel best in active environments. If your Moon sign is in Leo, you work well in leadership roles, but must be mindful to not come off as too bossy.

Magic to balance Moon in Leo:

- Sunbathe (while taking care to protect yourself from UV rays)
- Try beauty or glamor magic
- Repeat positive affirmations to yourself daily

LEO RISING SIGN

Leo Rising signs are attention seekers and natural performers. They are kind and influential people who naturally attract people into their sphere of influence. If your Rising sign is Leo, you have a warm persona and enjoy attention from others.

Magic to celebrate your Leo Rising:

- Throw a magically themed party
- Wear a magical cloak or clothing that makes you feel magical
- Participate in or attend the theater

VIRGO

- **Virgo Season:** August 23 to September 22
- **Symbol:** the Virgin
- **Ruling planet:** Mercury
- **Element:** earth
- **Colors:** brown, gray
- **Keywords:** analytical, intelligent, meticulous, observant, reliable
- **Magical correspondences:** dependability, earth magic, gaining information, independence, organization, restoring order, stability, thoughtfulness
- **Plants, herbs, resins, and essential oils:** almond, bergamot, broom, cornflower, eyebright, fennel, hazel, horehound, lavender, mint, moss, patchouli rosemary, skullcap, vervain
- **Crystals:** amazonite, apatite, celestite, diamond, fluorite, marble, moss agate, opal, sapphire, peridot
- **Tarot card:** the Hermit

CONJURING VIRGO ENERGY

The constellation of Virgo is associated with several goddesses from various cultural myths, including the Greek goddess of innocence and justice, Astraea, as well as Persephone (Greek) and Ceres (Roman), two goddesses associated with agriculture and the harvest. To the Babylonians, Virgo was Ishtar, the fertility goddess. These divine archetypes mirror the sign's caring, nurturing, and benevolent energy. Virgo's ruling planet, Mercury, emphasizes the more analytical attributes of this sign.

Virgos are known for being organized, orderly, and methodological in their tasks. They can be helpful and give great advice due to their practical nature. Virgo energy can be used to bring order into your world. It can also help with purification spells. Magical amulets and objects used to conjure Virgo energy include mojo bags, goddess statues or imagery, and pentacles.

VIRGO SUN SIGN

Those who have Virgo Sun are analytical, thoughtful, and meticulous in their routines. They are driven to do something meaningful that makes a difference in the world. It is important for Virgos to be mindful of being too critical about themselves and others. They can be influenced by gnome energy, feeling comfort with the patterns of growth in the green world around them.

Magic to highlight Virgo Sun:

- Study kitchen witchcraft and herbalism

- Create a vision board of your favorite magical imagery, spells, and quotes
- Wear a woodsy fragrance like patchouli

VIRGO MOON SIGN

Those with Moon in Virgo are brilliant perfectionists. They want to be surrounded by an organized environment, particularly one they've categorized themselves. While they may take an analytical, reserved approach to emotions, they are only doing so to better understand themselves and the world around them. If your Moon sign is Virgo, you must be mindful to watch your anxiety levels and take care of your nervous system.

Magic to balance Moon in Virgo:

- Work with building crystal grids
- Follow cooking recipes for healthy diets that are easy on the stomach
- Try breathwork to relax

VIRGO RISING SIGN

Virgo Rising signs appear to be reserved and hardworking. They have a strong worth ethic and like to be in service to others. Even though Virgo Rising signs are not the center of attention, they are keenly observant of everything going on around them. They are prone to worry, but you wouldn't be able to tell, as this Rising sign doesn't reveal their feelings too openly.

Magic to celebrate your Virgo Rising:

- Work for a company that supports people in need
- Take time alone to ground and find yourself
- Harvest herbs for holistic remedies

LIBRA

- **Libra Season:** September 23 to October 22. Libra begins on the Autumn Equinox (Mabon) in the Northern Hemisphere, and on the Spring Equinox (Ostara) in the Southern Hemisphere.
- **Symbol:** the Scales
- **Ruling planet:** Venus
- **Element:** air
- **Colors:** blue, pastels
- **Keywords:** affectionate, cooperative, diplomatic, peaceful, tender
- **Magical correspondences:** air magic, attraction, balance, beauty, calmness, compromise, equality, fairness, harmony, love, justice, partnership
- **Plants, herbs, resins, and essential oils:** catnip, clematis, lemon, lilac, magnolia, marjoram, mint, mullein, mugwort, orchid, passionflower, persimmon, rose, sweet pea, thyme, vanilla, violet
- **Crystals:** agate, aquamarine, ametrine, celestite, citrine, emerald, malachite, pink tourmaline, opal, rose quartz, sapphire
- **Tarot card:** Justice

CONJURING LIBRA ENERGY

Libra is associated with Themis, the Greek goddess of justice, order, and divine law. Themis was said to have taught the people the divine laws governing human behavior, to promote harmony within the family and community. She was also a prophetic goddess who presided over the Oracle of Delphi. Libra's divine feminine energies are aligned with its ruling planet, Venus. The word "Libra" is Latin for "weighing scales," symbolic of the balancing qualities of this sign.

Libras are known to be gentle, charming, caring, and affectionate people. They strive for harmony and balance in relationships and in their surroundings. Libra energy can be utilized to bring balance, justice, and worthiness into your life, and can also assist in helping to make decisions. Magical amulets and objects used to conjure Libra energy include scales, pendulums, and/or feathers.

LIBRA SUN SIGN

Those who have Libra Sun are affectionate, friendly, and diplomatic. Since Libra is represented by the scales, those with Sun in Libra are known to see "both sides of the story," and as result can be indecisive.

If your Sun sign is Libra, you are a loving and giving person, but must be mindful to stick up for yourself and remember your needs. Libras can be influenced by elf energy, demonstrating an appealing and wise demeanor that others feel intrigued by.

Magic to highlight Libra Sun:

- Spend the afternoon in a beautiful, old library
- Perform love spells
- Wear floral fragrances like orchid or sweet pea

LIBRA MOON SIGN

Those with Moon in Libra are kind truth seekers and advocates for others. They are emotionally intelligent people who feel most comfortable when they are surrounded by peace and quiet. They love beautiful things and enjoy spending time with their partners.

Magic to balance Moon in Libra:

- Listen to chimes or singing crystal bowls
- Go antique shopping
- Invite a friend over for tea and good conversation

LIBRA RISING SIGN

Libra Rising signs appear peaceful, hopeful, and playful. They can be stylish and attractive. They have good luck in social situations and keep hopes high for themselves and others. If your Rising sign is Libra, others feel relaxed and comfortable around you, opening up to you easily. However, it is important not to cave into people-pleasing tendencies.

Magic to celebrate your Libra Rising:

- Go to art therapy or try color magic
- Listen to or participate in a political debate
- Create a vision board representing your magical goals

SCORPIO

- **Scorpio Season:** October 23 to November 21. In the Wheel of the Year, the Scorpio season hosts Samhain in the Northern Hemisphere and Beltane in the Southern Hemisphere.
- **Symbol:** the Scorpion
- **Ruling planet:** Pluto
- **Element:** water
- **Colors:** black, burgundy
- **Keywords:** controlling, intense, lustful, mystical, psychological
- **Magical correspondences:** clairvoyance, change, divination, mysticism, occultism, passion, renewal, secrets, sex, water magic, wisdom
- **Plants, herbs, resins, and essential oils:** thistle, allspice, basil, blackthorn, cedar, chrysanthemum, geranium, hops, hellebore, myrrh, pomegranate, scorpion weed, thistle, wormwood, yew
- **Crystals:** black tourmaline, bloodstone, charoite, citrine, jet, obsidian, ruby, rutilated quartz, serpentine, yellow topaz

- **Tarot card:** Death

CONJURING SCORPIO ENERGY

According to Greek myth, Gaia created Scorpius (or Skorpios) the giant scorpion, and sent him to stop Orion from killing all the animals on earth. The scorpion stung Orion, and as a reward Gaia placed Scorpius in the sky, where he can be seen chasing Orion. This sign's energy is illustrated by scorpion symbolism, including death and rebirth, protection, personal power, and determination. Scorpio's ruling planets, Mars and Pluto, further enhance these energies.

Scorpios are known for their deep, intense, and mysterious nature. They have an intriguing relationship with their shadow sides, feeling drawn to issues below the surface, but also feeling challenged by intense moods. Scorpio energy can be used to heighten sex magic. Magical amulets and objects used to conjure Scorpic energy include scarab symbols, iron jewelry, and cauldrons.

SCORPIO SUN SIGN

Those who have Scorpio Sun are known to be intense, moody, and influential. They love deep conversations. Their interest in piercing below the surface can be intimidating to some, while others see Scorpio chats as a wonderful escape from small talk. They can be influenced by phoenix energy, and are said to experience many transformational phases in life, rising from the ashes to find a higher form of themselves.

Magic to highlight Scorpio Sun:

- Perform protection and/or water magic
- Study the intersection of mysticism and psychology
- Wear a fragrance that's spicy but protective, like cardamom or petitgrain

SCORPIO MOON SIGN

Those with Moon in Scorpio can be private and brooding. They love to be surrounded by intense imagery that reflects their unique opinions and preferences. If your Moon sign is Scorpio, you love deep conversations with intelligent people. You have a complex inner world, woven together by secrets and emotions.

Magic to balance Scorpio Moon:

- Practice banishment magic to release old emotions and move forward into new life
- Fill your home with intriguing art and antique amulets that speak to you on a deep level
- Work with a grief counselor

SCORPIO RISING SIGN

Scorpio Rising signs appear intense, powerful, and clever. They are willing to ask tough questions that require deep answers. They can lose their tempers quickly, and must be mindful not to self-sabotage or damage relationships due to anger or frustration.

Magic to celebrate your Scorpio Rising:

- Learn about or join a secret society
- Help others through transitory times
- Wear or carry ruby, citrine, sodalite, amethyst, or unakite

SAGITTARIUS

- **Sagittarius Season:** November 22 to December 21
- **Symbol:** the Archer
- **Ruling planet:** Jupiter
- **Element:** fire
- **Colors:** purple, gold, brown
- **Keywords:** animated, curious, energetic, independent, optimistic
- **Magical correspondences:** action, adventure, ambition, confidence, energy, enlightenment, extroversion, fire magic, friendliness, honesty, independence, motion, philosophy, travel, wisdom
- **Plants, herbs, resins, and essential oils:** anise, carnation, chestnut, chicory, copal, dahlia, dragon's blood, fig, frankincense, hibiscus, hydrangea, juniper, lime, marigold, oak, orange, peony, sassafras, red clover
- **Crystals:** amber, chrysolite, malachite, opal, sodalite, smoky quartz, turquoise, yellow jasper
- **Tarot card:** Temperance

CONJURING SAGITTARIUS ENERGY

The name Sagittarius comes from the Latin word for "archer," and the sign's symbol is an arrow. In Babylonian mythology, this constellation was associated with the war god Nergal, a centaur-like creature depicted with a bow and arrow. In Greek mythology, Sagittarius was associated with the wise and noble centaur Chiron, who was a teacher and mentor to many of the mythical heroes, and was said to have created the first celestial sphere. This sign's ruling planet is Jupiter, which aligns with the Sagittarian energies of wisdom and expansion.

Sagittarians are known for their adventurous qualities, seeking worldly exploration and philosophical conversations with a variety of people. They are glad to take risks or try new things to have the experience and expand their minds. Sagittarian energy can be used to assist in adventures, having fun, being more extrovertive, and speaking your mind. Magical amulets to conjure Sagittarius energy include antlers and arrowheads.

SAGITTARIUS SUN SIGN

Those who have Sagittarius Sun are known to be fun-loving and outgoing, seeking a world of adventure. They also are associated with philosophy, perhaps contemplating what they have observed in the exciting journeys they've been on.

It's important for Sagittarians to be careful not to get pushy or think their needs are above all others. They can be influenced by griffin energy, exploring the corners of the world and bringing their hopeful optimism wherever they go.

Magic to highlight Sagittarius Sun:

- Research and practice alchemy
- Study esoteric philosophers
- Travel to sacred destinations

SAGITTARIUS MOON SIGN

Those with Moon in Sagittarius are outspoken and happy-go-lucky. They love to be surrounded by souvenirs from their travels and crave freedom and independence. They love to give advice, but would do well to remember to listen and support other people's needs. If your Moon Sign is Sagittarius, you need to have excitement in your life and feel most comfortable when you can move around freely.

Magic to balance Sagittarius Moon:

- Try hot yoga
- Spend a day in a meditation center in a foreign country
- Study and experiment with chaos magic

SAGITTARIUS RISING SIGN

Sagittarius Rising signs are the life of the party, appearing as fun-loving free spirits. They are enthusiastic natural speakers and performers, and their humorous streak is great at cheering people up. If your Rising sign is Sagittarius, it is important to attempt to make deep and lasting connections with others, and not to make impulsive decisions.

Magic to celebrate your Sagittarius Rising:

- Try learning fire dancing, fire breathing, and/or belly dancing
- Have a bonfire with friends for an intimate story-telling time
- Host a drum circle

CAPRICORN

- **Capricorn Season:** December 22 to January 19. Capricorn begins on the Winter Solstice (Yule) in the Northern Hemisphere, and on the Summer Solstice (Litha) in the Southern Hemisphere.
- **Symbol:** the Goat
- **Ruling planet:** Saturn
- **Element:** earth
- **Colors:** charcoal, forest green, black, midnight blue
- **Keywords:** ambitious, careful, disciplined, protective, purposeful
- **Magical correspondences:** achievement, ambition, business, career, discipline, earth magic, endurance, grounding, longevity, manifestation, patience, productivity, purpose, responsibility, stability, security
- **Plants, herbs, resins, and essential oils:** barley, comfrey, cypress, elm, holly, honeysuckle, ivy, kale, musk, oak, oakmoss, patchouli, pine, rosemary, rowan, sorrel, vetiver, woodruff, yew
- **Crystals:** black tourmaline, coal, garnet, granite, malachite, obsidian, onyx, smoky quartz
- **Tarot card:** the Devil

CONJURING CAPRICORN ENERGY

The constellation Capricorn gets its name from the Latin translation of the Greek word for "goat-horned," and is associated with the mythical sea goat: a creature that is half fish, half goat, said to be able to swim the depths of the ocean and climb the highest mountain peaks. In one Greek myth, the god Pan, who was half-man and half-goat, jumped into a river to escape a giant beast and his lower body was transformed into a fish tail. Capricorn is ruled by Saturn, with its energies of discipline, rigidity, and responsibility.

Capricorns are known for their hard work ethic—they are determined, focused, and ambitious. They also have a dry sense of humor, and can bring a feeling of security into your life. Capricorn energy can be used to harness the endurance needed to work through tasks, chores, and major projects. Magical amulets and objects to conjure Capricorn energy include hag stones, worry stones, and salt.

CAPRICORN SUN SIGN

Those who have Capricorn Sun are known to be determined, disciplined, and responsible. They enjoy sticking to routines that they know will help lead to success. They love to have goals, not only related to professions, but also to peace of mind, stability, and praise from others.

Capricorns have a knack for being resourceful, but must learn how to open up to their feelings more. They can be influenced by Pan energy, which, while somewhat solitary, can bring growth and abundance into the world through their intense focus.

Magic to highlight Capricorn Sun:

- Dedicate yourself to a magical training through an online course or local mentor
- Practice prosperity and manifestation magic
- Wear an earthy fragrance like pine or oakmoss

CAPRICORN MOON SIGN

Those with Moon in Capricorn can be aloof, but this is to protect the inner environment they've built up in order to feel secure within. They love to be surrounded by items they find meaningful and comforting. If your Moon sign is Capricorn, you may not be revealing of your emotions, preferring to keep your feelings to yourself. While you work best with emotional solitude, allow those who are trustworthy to get to know the private you.

Magic to balance Capricorn Moon:

- Carry mojo bags for good luck
- Craft a charmed honey jar in your home for abundance
- Keep a weighted blanket on your bed

CAPRICORN RISING SIGN

Capricorn Rising signs can appear restricted, cold, and stiff. However, they are always prepared for anything, and their goal-driven determination can bring them a lot of success. If your Rising sign is Capricorn, be mindful to return to self-care and fun: not everything has to be work-related.

Magic to celebrate your Capricorn Rising:

- Help others with success and money magic
- Give a gift of gratitude to someone you care about
- Go for a long hike in the woods or along a shoreline

AQUARIUS

- **Aquarius Season:** January 20 to February 18. In the Wheel of the Year, the Aquarius season hosts Imbolc in the Northern Hemisphere and Lughnasadh in the Southern Hemisphere.
- **Symbol:** the Water Bearer
- **Ruling planet:** Uranus
- **Element:** air
- **Colors:** aquamarine blue, ultramarine blue, indigo, turquoise
- **Keywords:** clever, eccentric, innovative, inquisitive, rebellious
- **Magical correspondences:** acceptance, air magic, charity, cleverness, creativity, freedom, hope, humor, independence, individuality, inspiration, innovative thinking, knowledge
- **Plants, herbs, resins, and essential oils:** acacia, benzoin, bistort, chive, citron, dogwood, iris, gum mastic, lavender, lemon verbena, peppermint, pine, rosemary, rowan, sage, sandalwood, snowdrop, star anise

- **Crystals:** aquamarine, amethyst, angelite, celestite, chalcedony, crystal quartz, fluorite, labradorite, lapis lazuli, star sapphire
- **Tarot card:** the Star

CONJURING AQUARIUS ENERGY

The name Aquarius is Latin for "water bearer," and this constellation is associated with a Greek shepherd boy, Ganymede, who was abducted by Zeus on account of his unusual beauty and made a cupbearer for the gods. As a gift for his service, Zeus gave him eternal youth and immortality. Although the symbol for this sign depicts two waves of water, Aquarius is an air sign, ruled by both Saturn and Uranus. The combined energies of these two planets—discipline and freedom, responsibility and disruption—align with the unique and quirky traits of this sign.

Aquarians are known for being eccentric and uniquely individualist, and dancing to the beat of their own drum. They celebrate weirdness, and are more than happy to ask questions that help to reveal fresh perspectives. Aquarius energy can be used in magic for awakening radical ideas, finding freedom from unpleasant situations, and inspiring creative thinking. Magical amulets and objects used to conjure the magic of Aquarius include divining rods, bells, and vases.

AQUARIUS SUN SIGN

Those who have Aquarius Sun are said to be innovative, unique, creative, and quirky. While their nature is fun and eccentric, they can also be unpredictable and impractical.

If your Sun sign is Aquarius, you love a weird conversation that takes you down an intellectual rabbit hole. Be mindful of how you can open up to others more. Aquarians can be influenced by slyph energy, the beautiful essence of the element of air, helping others to awaken the potential of their minds.

Magic to highlight Aquarius Sun:

- Work closely with a coven or other forms of group magic
- Study astrology
- Wear a peaceful fragrance like lavender or sandalwood

AQUARIUS MOON SIGN

Those with Moon in Aquarius are dynamic, may be interested in activism, and are philosophically minded. They are natural problem solvers and come up with innovative solutions, thanks to their ability to "see the big picture." If your Moon sign is Aquarius, you may feel like an outsider, but must learn to accept and celebrate your unique ways, as you are bringing refreshing progress to the world.

Magic to balance Aquarius Moon:

- Light incense in your home

- Offer a safe space of acceptance to others and create safe space within your own home
- Decorate with fairy lights and star patterns

AQUARIUS RISING SIGN

Aquarius Rising signs appear as eccentric, unconventional, and progressive. They are incredibly smart individuals who want to make "peace and love" a real thing in this world and in their lives. If your Rising sign is Aquarius, you are talented at helping others and uncovering new ideas to make things better.

Magic to celebrate your Aquarius Rising:

- Do volunteer work for an organization or cause that is important to you
- Start and run a magical meetup group
- Wear or carry aquamarine, sapphire, moonstone, or clear quartz

PISCES

- **Pisces Season:** February 19 to March 20
- **Symbol:** Two fish
- **Ruling planet:** Neptune
- **Element:** water
- **Colors:** aqua, indigo, turquoise, sea green
- **Keywords:** calming, dreamy, empathetic, idealistic, poetic
- **Magical correspondences:** art, compassion, empathy, endings and new beginnings, forgiveness, healing work, imagination, lucid dreams, peacefulness, psychic work, romance, telepathy, unification
- **Plants, herbs, resins, and essential oils:** aloe, catnip, eucalyptus, fig, gardenia, hyacinth, jasmine, lemon, lilac, mugwort, peach, rue, sandalwood, sweet pea, water lily, willow
- **Crystals:** amethyst, aquamarine, jade, moonstone, mother-of-pearl, sapphire, sugilite, turquoise
- **Tarot card:** the Moon

CONJURING PISCES ENERGY

The constellation Pisces is associated with Aphrodite and her son Eros, who transformed into two fish to escape the monster Typhon. (In another version, they were rescued by two fish who carried them to safety.) The zodiac glyph for this sign depicts two fish swimming in opposite directions, connected by a horizontal band, which may symbolize the push and pull of the psychic tides of Piscean energy. Jupiter and Neptune, the ruling planets of Pisces, embody this water sign's creativity and compassion, as well as its tendencies toward fantasy and escapism.

As the final sign in the zodiac wheel, Pisces have a reflective quality, mirroring back what you reveal to them. They are known for their sensitive, dreamy, idealistic nature. Piscean energy can be used to awaken psychic abilities, enhance vivid dreams, and move through sensitive feelings and events. Magical amulets and objects used to conjure the magic of Pisces include sea glass, nautiluses, and sea stars.

PISCES SUN SIGN

Those who have Pisces Sun are said to be intuitive, dreamy, and idealistic. This mystical Sun placement emphasizes sensitivity and introspection, but Pisces must be mindful that they are not responsible for fixing everything. They can be influenced by undine energy, which is friendly, emotional, and desires to help others.

Magic to highlight Pisces Sun:

- Practice divination of any kind

- Study dream work and astral projection
- Wear a dreamy fragrance like jasmine or gardenia

PISCES MOON SIGN

Those with Moon in Pisces are sensitive and compassionate. They feel comfortable being surrounded by flowing materials and water. This is a strong placement for psychic abilities, and Pisceans are prone to being dreamy. If your Moon sign is Pisces, you will need a safe space that serves as a retreat from the harsh outside world.

Magic to balance Pisces Moon:

- Blend love and healing potions
- Read and/or write poetry
- Create a comfortable space at home for you to relax and share with trusted friends

PISCES RISING SIGN

Pisces Rising signs appear vulnerable and sensitive, being easily influenced by other peoples' energy. They come off as spacey, but this is because they are sweet and sentimental daydreamers. If your Rising sign is Pisces, you must work extra hard to protect your feelings from being hurt.

Magic to celebrate your Pisces Rising:

- Do healing magic for others
- Go to a healing spa retreat
- Become a certified yoga instructor or reiki practitioner

ZODIAC SIGN REFLECTIONS

These are questions you can reflect on in a journal, draw about, or even approach in meditation.

First, fill in the blanks for the following sentences:

- My Sun Sign is _____. Therefore, I am _____. I have the potential to be _____.
- My Moon Sign is _____. Therefore, I feel _____. I find I am the most comfortable when _____.
- My Rising Sign is _____. Therefore, I appear _____. Others appreciate that I am _____.

Now, contemplate the following questions:

- What about your Sun sign description do you agree with? Are there characteristics related to this placement that you do not resonate with?
- If you could have any Sun sign, what would it be and why? How can you use magic from that sign to bring more confidence and opportunity into your life?

- What about your Moon sign description do you agree with? Are there characteristics related to this placement that you do not resonate with?

- If you could have any Moon sign, what would it be and why? How can you use magic from that sign to bring comfort and ease into your world?

- What about your Rising sign description do you agree with? Are there characteristics related to this placement that you do not resonate with?

- If you could have any Rising sign, what would it be and why? How can you use magic from that sign to attract success and pleasure into your life?

Chapter Four:
THE MYSTICAL MOON: LUNAR PHASES AND MOVEMENT THROUGH THE SIGNS

Our beautiful luminary in the night sky, the mystical Moon, moves quickly, entering into a new sign roughly every two and half days. The moon orbits the earth in 27.3 days, and its phases cycle every 29.5 days. This pace of orbit means that the moon's motion, which sways and influences the tides, also subtly sways and influences our emotional inner worlds on a very regular basis.

This chapter will examine the moon's cyclical phases as well as its movements through the signs, to assist you in understanding their energies, moods, and magic.

LUNAR PHASES

The lunar phases refer to the portion of the moon we see illuminated from our perspective on Earth. There are eight phases, all of which offer different energies, magical correspondences, and astrological opportunities. Each lunar phase allows you the opportunity to focus on various intentions, set goals in your life, practice awareness of your thoughts and moods, and take time for self-development and growth.

In *Cosmic Health*, author Jennifer Racioppi says of the moon: "... like you, she remains herself, even as she changes. The moon's cyclical nature exemplifies how to move from darkness to light while journeying through different experiences each time."

NEW MOON

The New Moon is a time associated with new beginnings, starting new routines, and considering fresh perspectives. During the New Moon, direct your magic towards new ideas, new goals, beneficial changes, welcoming in blessings from the universe, and initiating projects. This is a time of "beginner's luck," so take a chance on something that means a lot to you.

To enhance your connection to the New Moon:

- Try something new that you've always wanted to do but haven't tried before
- Consider what you are feeling called to do with your life
- Think about new goals, new projects, and positive routines you'd like to start
- Wear white clothing and labradorite jewelry

WAXING CRESCENT

The Waxing Crescent is a growing moon; therefore, it is associated with gathering information and taking initial steps toward a goal. Take the ideas that you conjured during the New Moon and begin to strategize and construct methods to bring your dreams into reality. During the Waxing Crescent Moon, direct your magic towards growth, healing, increasing overall wellness, and building abundance. Think of this phase as a time to metaphorically "plant seeds," and plot out paths to success.

To enhance your connection to the Waxing Crescent Moon:

- Take the list you created during the New Moon and build out plans to reaching those goals
- Consider what next steps are you excited to take
- Wear pale green clothing and green aventurine jewelry
- Create positive affirmations and repeat them often
- Design and draw a sigil

FIRST QUARTER
(OR THE WAXING QUARTER)

The First Quarter is still a building phase, and is therefore associated with further growing momentum. This is a time when you must remain focused on the projects at hand and consider what other resources need to be pulled in for continued progress. You can use the First Quarter to direct your magic towards success spells, making choices that bring you good luck, and uncovering the best options. This is a good time to make changes that help you focus and manage your time better. It is a transitory phase where you can build upon your "Plan A," but also develop a "Plan B."

To enhance your connection to the First Quarter Moon:

- Wear emerald green clothing and wear malachite
- Consider where you are on your goal's timeline
- Do a money spell – especially auspicious on a Sunday, Thursday, or when the Moon is in Taurus.

WAXING GIBBOUS

At the Waxing Gibbous we are coming closer and closer to the Full Moon and a time of fruition. Waxing Gibbous energy is excellent for students and researchers who wish to collect, analyze, and refine information. At this point, magic can be directed to encouragement, courage, hope, and energy. You can also use this time to adjust and modify the projects that you are working on. This phase is all about perseverance and knowing that completion is coming closer and closer.

To enhance your connection to the Waxing Gibbous Moon:

- Do a meditation to remember patience
- Ask friends to check in with you and hold you accountable on your goals
- Drink Yerba Matte or coffee
- Wear teal or turquoise clothes and turquoise or celestite jewelry

FULL MOON

The Full Moon is a time of fullness as well as completion. At this point, magic can be directed to fulfillment of wishes, creativity, transformation, and fertility. This is also said to be a time of heightened magic and psychic abilities, so you can consider doing any kind of spell work and divination during the Full Moon.

To enhance your connection to the Full Moon:

- Wear white or silver clothes and selenite or moonstone jewelry
- Attend an Esbat ritual that honors the divine and cyclical nature of the moon
- Charge your crystals and magical tools in the moonlight
- Make Full Moon Water (see instructions toward the end of this chapter)
- Practice any form of divination that calls to you

WANING GIBBOUS
(DISSEMINATING MOON)

The Waning Gibbous phase is a time of sharing, expression, and being in community. This is considered a good time to exchange abundance from the Full Moon with others, whether that is a material or energetic gift. At this point, magic can be directed towards communication, friendship, gratitude, and protection. Since this is a waning phase, it is an excellent time to finish tasks and review the growth you've experienced during the previous phases of the current lunar cycle.

To enhance your connection to the Waning Gibbous Moon:

- Clean your home, both physically and energetically
- Consider how you feel emotionally at the end of projects and phases in your life
- Host a small friendly gathering
- Wear gray or silver clothes and crystal quartz jewelry

THIRD QUARTER
(WANING QUARTER)

The Third Quarter is when we release what has culminated over the previous lunar phases, and in doing so, make room for new opportunities. At this point magic can be directed toward release, banishment, gratitude, owning up to your actions, and letting go of things that no longer serve you. In this phase we can make resolutions and conclusions.

To enhance your connection to the Third Quarter Moon:

- Wear black clothes and black tourmaline or jet jewelry
- Cleanse your crystals and magical tools in a bowl with sea salt
- Purify your home by burning herbs and/or incense
- Clear your home of any clutter and/or sweep with a magical besom

WANING CRESCENT

The Waning Crescent Moon is a time of endings, pause, reflection, and rest. We take this time to consider the events that have occurred over the past lunar cycle, what has entered our life, and what has left our life. At this point, magic can be directed towards recuperation, self-love, peace, and wisdom.

To enhance your connection to the Waning Crescent Moon:

- Write in your journal about what you have done over this lunar cycle
- Review your calendar and ensure you have time to pause and unplug for a little while
- Do something easygoing like cozying up with a book or a funny TV show
- Wear indigo or deep purple clothes and lapis lazuli

THE MOON'S MOVEMENT THROUGH THE ZODIAC SIGNS

Each celestial body's movement through a zodiac sign is known in astrology as a "transit."

The Moon transits quickly through the zodiac signs—typically every two or two and a half days—and its presence within each sign creates subtle energies that can influence us from day to day. We can also use these times for setting magical intentions or doing specific spiritual work in line with the astrological energy.

MOON IN ARIES

This is an energizing time when you feel excited and spontaneous. Moon in Aries is an excellent time to start new projects, create new goals, and take on challenges. Fill in your planner with appointments and check-ins and take this time to work on shorter projects.

Do magic during this time to begin new projects, work on confidence, and start new chapters in your life. Be mindful that you may get irritated or agitated more easily during this transit. Follow your heart and see where your gut instincts suggest you move towards.

MOON IN TAURUS

This is a grounding time that feels secure, abundant, and full of opportunity to grow. Moon in Taurus feels stabilizing and is a good time to work on practical matters like chores and finances.

This is an excellent time to do magic for love, self-care, sensuality, prosperity, and protection. This is also a good time to go on a date. Be mindful not to overspend or overindulge during this transit. Slow and steady wins the race during Taurus Moon.

MOON IN GEMINI

This is a thoughtful time when you feel your mind running in different directions with clever and innovative ideas. Moon in Gemini can be a wonderful time to go on business trips, do communication magic, tell jokes, read, and write.

In addition to communication magic, try spellwork for collaboration and/or wisdom under a Gemini Moon. While this is a wonderful time to speak your mind through conversation and writing, be mindful about gossip or distractions during this transit. If you are feeling restless, take a break with a good book.

MOON IN CANCER

This is a sensitive time when your focus goes into your moods and any empathic sensations you may be picking up on. As a result, you may feel inclined to stay home and be gentle while you work through tender emotions.

Your psychic awareness and intuition may be heightened during this transit, so pay attention to any psychic messages you sense. Cast spells for vivid dreams and practice divination. This is also a good time to work on healing, home spells, and building your self-esteem. Be mindful about mood swings, clinginess, or hypersensitivity during this time.

MOON IN LEO

This is a bold time when you are feeling boisterous and confident. Moon in Leo is a wonderful time to enjoy something entertaining and ride the wave of empowered confidence you are feeling. If you are feeling creative during this transit, take the time to express it.

If you are feeling flirtatious, muster up your courage and share your feelings in a loving, playful, and respectful manner. Try love or creativity magic during the Leo Moon. Be mindful of becoming overdramatic or bossy during this time.

MOON IN VIRGO

This is an analytical time when you feel called to organize and refine your world. Moon in Virgo is an excellent opportunity to review your health and wellness, as well as clean up any clutter in your home.

This is also a good time for herbal magic, healing spells, and job-related spells. You will find your focus is strong during this transit, so use it to your advantage and get things done, but be mindful of perfectionism or tendencies to micromanage.

MOON IN LIBRA

This is an affectionate time when you are focused on partnership, compatibility, cooperation, balance, and speaking your truth. Libra Moon is an excellent time to do vision board magic or scrapbook magic, as well as beauty and love spells.

It can also be spent celebrating any type of partnership, including business partners and loyal friends. Be mindful of indecisiveness during this transit.

MOON IN SCORPIO

This is an intense time when you are exploring your deepest emotions and reviewing your secrets. You may feel extra passionate or overly emotional during the Scorpio Moon, making it an ideal time to explore your inner world and dust off the skeletons in your closet, perhaps with the help of a therapist.

It is also an excellent time for sex magic. You may also use this time to do banishment magic to remove bad habits, bad relationships, obsessions, and fixations. Be mindful of possessiveness or jealousy during this transit.

MOON IN SAGITTARIUS

This is an exploratory time where you are feeling adventurous and curious. You may feel inclined to play sports, watch sports, or do something extra active during this time. The Sagittarius Moon is an excellent time to travel, do something playfully spontaneous, and reconnect with whatever you find fun to participate in.

Try attending a drum circle or dance class during this time to release your magical energy through movement. This is a good time to perform good luck spells, road opener spells, and expansion spells. Be mindful of speaking out of line or being brash during this transit.

MOON IN CAPRICORN

The Capricorn Moon has a more serious energy and is a good time to stay practical in your approach to projects. This is an ambitious time when you are feeling a call to "get the job done."

If you keep yourself disciplined during this transit, your efforts will result in success. Moon in Capricorn is an excellent time to perform career, employment, abundance, and prosperity spells. Be mindful of remaining friendly and not skipping well-earned breaks.

MOON IN AQUARIUS

This is an innovative time where you are feeling social, unconventional, and idealistic. You may feel extra inquisitive and want to engage with the world around you.

This is a wonderful time to meet with covens, go to group therapy sessions, or find outlets for artistic expression. If you have any original ideas during this time, be sure to jot them down! Consider working magic to make your life easier or helping you to see fresh perspectives, but be mindful not to make radical changes during this transit.

MOON IN PISCES

This is a spiritual time when your psychic abilities may be heightened, and you feel a need to return to spiritual and/or mellow activities. If you are feeling dreamy, take the time to meditate, write poetry, or relax in a hot bath.

This is an excellent time to perform peaceful, calming, intuitive magic. Practice with your divination tools and record any psychic premonitions you have or omens you observe. Be mindful of spacing out or taking things too personally during this transit.

VOID MOON

If you are using an astrological almanac or listen frequently to astrology podcasts, you may come across the term "void moon," or "void of course." This term has slightly different definitions in different schools of astrology. Generally speaking, however, the Moon goes void-of-course when it has completed its final aspect with another planet, just before moving into a new sign.

These occasions are considered to be quiet times, when it is best to pause, and refrain from making major decisions, going to big events, or pushing through major projects. These void moons do not last for too long—sometimes only a few hours—and are a great time to rest, spend time alone, or just generally take a break. Some excellent activities to consider during the void moon include meditation, restorative yoga, reiki, journaling, napping, and breathwork.

SPECIAL MOONS

There are unique lunar experiences that occur less frequently and offer special, heightened magical opportunities and lessons.

Blue Moon: A Blue Moon is the second full moon within one calendar month. A Blue Moon is said to be an extra magical time and an especially good time to perform spells and divination. It is an excellent occasion for working beneficial magic, absorbing lunar energy, and communing with lunar deities.

Black Moon: A Black Moon is the second new moon within one calendar month. The Black Moon is said to be an intense time that can be used for banishment spells, releasing old patterns, cleansing and purificction magic, and shadow work.

Super Moon: A Super Moon is a full moon which is at the point in its orbit that is nearest to the Earth, making it appear larger in the night sky. Astrologically, Super Moons are said to create intense energy for change, so things that are worth releasing from your life may make themselves apparent during this time. Super Moons are also said to be a time when emotions, psychic awareness, and magical abilities have an extra boost. If a Super Moon is coming up for you, locate the sign the Moon is in to gather more information about what energies may be intensified and enhanced during this time.

FULL MOON WATER

It is believed that moonlight has magical energy. Many people will leave their crystals, magical tools, and divination tools in moonlight to purify and recharge them with divine, feminine energy. Water can also be left under the light of the Full Moon to charge, and then used for a variety of magical purposes. For example, charged Full Moon Water can cleanse magical tools and magical spaces. If you are using purified water, you can also drink it to enhance psychic abilities, or wash with it to enhance beauty.

All you need to do to make Full Moon Water is take purified water outside in a clean and clear glass container and allow it to sit in the moonlight for at least an hour or two. If you like, place a crystal quartz and/or moonstone in the container as well. If you leave the jar out overnight, retrieve it in the morning and place it on your altar.

LUNAR CALENDAR JOURNALING EXERCISE

You can use the following exercise to help you work with the magic and energies of both the current lunar phase and its location in the sky. Using an almanac, determine the current phase of the moon and the sign the moon is moving through. Then fill in the following sentences:

- The current lunar phase is _____. For me, this means the energy of the Moon is focused on _____.

- The Moon is currently in the sign of _____. For me, this means my magic can be directed toward _____.

- I am currently feeling _____. This resonates with the current lunar phase because _____.

- I am feeling called to focus on _____ during this Moon's movement and can do _____ magic to support this.

LUNAR PHASE DIVINATION SPREAD

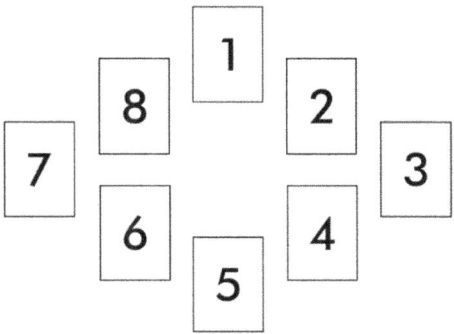

This divination spread can be used with tarot cards, oracle cards, or other divination sets such as runes. There are two ways that you can utilize this spread. The first approach will show you events, lessons, and/or magical manifestations that will unfold during the next lunar cycle. The second is to perform the reading when you are ready to start a new project or phase in your life.

Lunar Cycle Reading

Begin by charting out the dates of each upcoming lunar phase. Then perform this reading on the New Moon, using the first card as the current events card. Each subsequent card will chart out events, lessons, and magic that will occur around the date of the corresponding lunar phase.

- **Card One:** Current events at the New Moon
- **Card Two:** Events at the Waxing Crescent
- **Card Three:** Events at the First Quarter
- **Card Four:** Events at the Waxing Gibbous
- **Card Five:** Events at the Full Moon
- **Card Six:** Events at the Waning Gibbous
- **Card Seven:** Events at the Third Quarter
- **Card Eight:** Events at the Waning Crescent

<u>**New Project Reading**</u>

The second way to read this spread is to perform the reading when you are ready to start a new phase in your life. You can do this reading whenever you're ready to explore the best projects and goals to dive into next.

Note that the timing of the unfolding will not necessarily line up with the phases of the lunar cycle—these positions are related to the corresponding energies of each lunar phase with respect to manifestation. Use the following interpretations for each card:

- **Card One (New Moon):** New projects, routines, or goals that you should start to focus on now
- **Card Two (Waxing Crescent):** Plans to make those new projects come into reality and first steps in the project

- **Card Three (Third Quarter):** Magic and other activities to do to bring good luck and success to this project
- **Card Four (Waxing Gibbous):** Ways to stay motivated and energized with the project, and opportunities for improvement
- **Card Five (Full Moon):** Ways that this project will come into fruition, and how it will look when it is completed
- **Card Six (Waning Gibbous):** How the world will receive this project, and response from others for your efforts
- **Card Seven (Third Quarter):** Lessons learned from the project, and what you can do better next time
- **Card Eight (Waning Crescent):** How to rest and recuperate after the project is completed

Chapter Five: OUR MAGICAL SKIES: SPECIAL CELESTIAL EVENTS

Astrology embodies more than just signs and stars—special celestial events in the skies can also influence our magic, our personal moods, and world events.

This chapter will briefly explore the phenomena of solar and lunar eclipses, planetary retrogrades, comets, and meteor showers, to see how they can influence the world around you and the magic inside of you.

SOLAR AND LUNAR ECLIPSES

Eclipses are potent astrological events. The ancients largely feared eclipses, as they tended to correlate with catastrophes like earthquakes and floods. In general, eclipses can bring surprise events and mark big changes. Their energies are not exactly easy to deal with, but they can result in growth and positive change if you keep an open mind.

Solar eclipses take place during new moons when the moon moves between the sun and Earth. In the case of a partial solar eclipse, only part of the sun will be dark. During a total solar eclipse, the sun looks completely blackened out, with a spectacular bright ring around the edge. Lunar eclipses take place during full moons when the Earth moves between the sun and the moon. The sun's light over the moon during a lunar eclipse gives it a mystical, blood-red hue.

Because they tend to be related to unstable energy, some practitioners will avoid doing magic during a solar eclipse. However, others look at it as a unique, sometimes a once-in-a-lifetime opportunity to take care of unfinished business, push through major blockages, consider new perspectives, and plant intentions for the future.

Likewise, some will opt to skip spell work during a lunar eclipse, due to the intense energies and potential for drastic change. On the other hand, some see lunar eclipses as an excellent time for transformative shadow work, divination, meditation, and banishment magic.

The zodiac sign where an eclipse occurs will influence the specific energies of the event. For example, a solar eclipse in Aries is particularly fiery, outward-focused, and action-oriented, whereas in Cancer, the focus is more on changes within the home and family. To start recognizing and understanding the energies of solar and lunar eclipses, take note in your journal of your moods and experiences during these events.

PLANETS IN RETROGRADE

Planets are described as being in retrograde when they appear to be moving backwards from the perspective of Earth. This is an illusion, however, caused by the distance and speed of the planet's orbit in relation to the Earth. In general, retrograde periods are often considered astrological rough patches. Mercury in retrograde in particular gets blamed for many mishaps, and has a notorious reputation for causing communication breakdowns, travel snags, and electronic fiascos.

Retrograde times are not all doom and gloom, however. For one thing, they are more common than many people realize, as most of the time we have at least one planet, if not several, in retrograde. Each planet goes retrograde at least once in a while, some for longer periods than others, each generating different astrological influences. The retrogrades of inner planets—those closest to the sun—tend to have stronger effects on individual lives, while the outer planets are more influential on a societal or global level.

The effects of a retrograde are typically more strongly felt at the beginning and the end of the retrograde period. For the longer retrogrades of the outer planets, the days surrounding the start date are an ideal time to consider the suggestions below, while the days toward the end of the retrograde are an opportunity to reflect on any lessons or significant developments that occurred during the retrograde phase.

MERCURY RETROGRADE

Mercury Retrograde occurs three or four times every year. It is dreaded by many people, largely due to attention-grabbing headlines in the days leading up to each Mercury Retrograde, painting this time as a harbinger of mishaps.

This retrograde is associated with communication issues, travel problems, electronic malfunctions, and delays of all kinds. While this *can* be the case, it isn't the only aspect of this retrograde. This is also a time where you can consider how to communicate clearly and effectively. Typos and errors happen at this time, so be mindful to slow down and not hit "send" without re-reading emails and Tweets first!

Mercury Retrograde also helps you to be detail-oriented in planning. The phrase "setting yourself up for success" is perfect to keep in mind at Mercury Retrograde, when it's a good idea to have a Plan A and a Plan B. If possible, keep from starting new projects or signing contracts during Mercury Retrograde.

In general, take this time to reflect humbly, listen quietly, observe mindfully, and prepare diligently for all outcomes. To help you maintain this approach throughout the retrograde period, you may want to set up a Mercury Retrograde altar, which is explained later in this chapter.

VENUS RETROGRADE

Venus Retrograde occurs every 18 months and is said to impact relationships and romance.

You may find that you are thinking about past relationships, repeating mistakes from past relationships, or experiencing familiar challenges with romance during this time. This allows you the opportunity to uncover any underlying issues with how you approach relationships and learn lessons so as to not repeat them again.

This is an excellent time to contemplate and practice self-love, be gentle with partners, and practice forgiveness. This period is also an ideal time to contemplate what brings you deep, authentic joy. If there are things in your life (including relationships) that are keeping you from growing and evolving, it is time to remove them. Avoid overspending during this time and monitor finances closely.

MARS RETROGRADE

Mars Retrograde occurs about once every two years.

During this time, you may feel irritable, cranky, and easily frustrated. Even worse, you may have low energy, low libido, and no motivation to do anything about it.

Mars Retrograde is an excellent time to review your priorities: since you have less physical energy, your true priorities will be where you put your mental attention. Pause before reacting to ensure that you do not act out of spite or annoyance.

JUPITER RETROGRADE

Jupiter is in retrograde for about a third of the year.

While Jupiter is in retrograde, you may feel like you must work harder to keep good fortune in your life.

During Jupiter Retrograde, take moments to reflect on when you've had cycles of luck and growth in your life, considering what it is you had to do to get to that point of success.

SATURN RETROGRADE

Saturn is in retrograde for about a third of the year.

Saturn Retrograde offers us a little relief from heavy obligations and intense restrictions.

Use this time to complete old tasks you have been procrastinating that need to be done once and for all.

URANUS RETROGRADE

Uranus is in retrograde for about 22 weeks every year.

During this retrograde you may feel trapped, as if you cannot make progress as effectively as you'd wish.

This retrograde asks you to reconsider patterns in your life and how you got "unstuck" in other stagnant phases. You may also feel a little antisocial during this retrograde, so it is a good time to reflect on your personal uniqueness and your favorite solitary activities.

NEPTUNE RETROGRADE

Neptune is in retrograde for about 23 weeks every year.

Neptune Retrograde can make you feel a little foggy, as if you are not completely present and drifting off into space. Your intuition may not be as easy to tap into and you may experience strange sleeping patterns.

During this retrograde there are lessons to be uncovered about your fantasy world and illusions or dreams that may reveal where you escape reality. Honor your imagination by determining if those fantasies are worth shifting into the real world.

PLUTO RETROGRADE

Pluto is in retrograde for about 186 days every year!

Pluto Retrograde is a good time to think about monumental personal changes that shift and transform your life.

Retrograde periods are wonderful times to pause, reflect, and learn lessons. Think of retrogrades as opportunities to find new, innovative approaches and to move away from outdated patterns. After all, no matter what's happening in the skies, life must go on!

MERCURY IN RETROGRADE ALTAR SET UP

Many people feel wary when they hear we are moving into a Mercury Retrograde season. While they are common and can be manageable, this is a suggested list of things you can arrange on your altar to assist in ensuring a smooth and easy-flowing Mercury Retrograde.

- **An image of the Magician tarot card:** The Magician is connected to Mercury energy, representing communication, learning, and action. The Magician can assist you with keeping your thoughts, words, and actions clear through Mercury Retrograde.

- **A living plant that is associated with Mercury:** Allow the energy of Mercury to thrive and grow on your altar with plants such as lavender, rosemary, peppermint, or thyme.

- **Incense associated with Mercury:** Burn incense with benzoin, gum mastic, frankincense, and/or rosemary to help purify your sacred space and stimulate mental agility, support concentration, and awaken spiritual awareness. You can also use the Mercury Incense Blend recipe from Chapter 2.

- **An image or statue of the god Mercury:** If you feel like it, leave petitions for clarity, safe travels, speedy delivery, and smooth transactions with Mercury. Leave him offerings of almonds, hazelnuts, star anise, drawings of the Mercury glyph, lit yellow candles, images of the caduceus, or amulets shaped like wings.

- **Mercury-corresponding crystals:** Dress your altar with crystals that are associated with the planet Mercury, such as hematite, mica, or muscovite. While the element known as mercury is poisonous and should never be used, you can still represent it with a jar of water mixed with silver glitter, ink, and/or dye.

COMETS AND METEOR SHOWERS IN ASTROLOGY

While the planets and luminaries understandably get most of astrology's attention, there are other cosmic mysteries passing through the night skies that are worth exploring when the opportunity arises: comets and meteors.

Visible comets are fairly rare occurrences, with a major comet becoming visible from Earth once every 5 to 10 years, on average. Meteors can be seen on almost any dark night, if you happen to be looking in the right place at the right time, but they are particularly easy to see during meteor showers (more on this below).

Comets are large, icy conglomerates of dust and gasses, typically found in the outer reaches of the solar system. We see them when they get close enough to the sun to begin evaporating from the sun's heat, and this process creates the bright tail we observe from Earth.

Historically, comets have had an ominous feeling to them, being harbingers of uneasy challenges and major events. Astrologically, they can expose grief, pushing you to work with more difficult emotions to release yourself from pain. Because their visibility is caused by their breaking down in the sun's heat, comets are also thought to help remove blockages and release old energies that no longer serve us.. As the comets move onwards, so can we.

Meteors are much smaller, broken-off pieces of either comets, asteroids, or planetoids. They are known as "meteoroids" until they collide with the atmosphere of a planet, at which point they are considered meteors. The flash they give off when burning up in the planet's atmosphere is why they are often called "shooting stars."

Like comets, meteor showers have been considered astrological markers for significant events, though they do not have as heavy of an energy as comets do. They bring in transformative energy, awakening bright ideas and innovative plans. Meteor showers may offer a time where you can change course to reposition yourself on a path you'd prefer.

METEOR SHOW MAGIC THROUGH THE YEAR

A meteor shower occurs when the Earth's orbit passes through the trail of debris from a comet. These are typically named for the stars or constellations they appear close to when we see them.

There are annual meteor showers that deliver beautiful night sky shows every single year. If you would like to incorporate magic into these special occasions, be on the lookout for exact dates and timing for the following annual showers:

- **Quadrantids:** This meteor shower takes place in January, seen near the constellation Bootes, which includes a smaller constellation once known as Quadrans Muralis. This ancient constellation has the shape of a human torso, and was named by the Greek astronomer Ptolemy from the word "plowman" or "ox driver." During this meteor shower, perform work-related magic related to relieving burnout and bringing clarity to work situations.

- **Lyrids:** The Lyrids shower takes place in April, seen near the constellations Lyra and Hercules. The harp-shaped constellation Lyra is associated with the myth of Orpheus, who was gifted the beautiful harp from the god Apollo. This constellation also contains one of the brightest and closest stars to us, Vega, which is also known as the "Harp star." To work with the energies of the Lyrids shower, perform magic related to healing with sound and art and transforming grief into creative expression.

- **Perseids:** This is the brightest annual meteor shower, and is active around mid-July through mid-August, seen near the constellation Perseus. This constellation is associated with the Greek hero Perseus, who killed the monster Medusa. To harness the energies of this shower, perform magic related to overcoming inner demons and protecting yourself from potential unfriendly "monsters" in the world.

- **Orionids:** This meteor shower takes place in October, seen near the constellation Orion, named for the Greek hunter. Orion is most notable in the sky for his bright belt of three stars in row. Orion's Belt has been honored and observed by several ancient cultures. Perform magic during this time to connect with ancient wisdom, and draw on Orion's energy for empowerment magic.

- **Taurids:** This meteor shower takes place in November, seen near the constellation Taurus. This is an excellent time for Taurus-related magic, working to regenerate health, wellness, beauty, and pleasure in your life.

- **Leonids:** This Leonids shower takes place in November, seen near the constellation Leo. Perform Leo-related magic during this shower to revive joy, creativity, and fun in your life.
- **Geminids:** This meteor shower takes place in December, seen near the constellation Gemini. This is an excellent time for Gemini-related magic to assist with researching, updating plans, and revising written projects, and goals related to travel.

WISH UPON A STAR BAY LEAF SPELL

Greek astronomer Ptolemy believed that shooting stars were signs of the gods watching from heaven, and therefore provided an opportunity to make a wish that the gods were more likely hear and grant.

This spell harnesses the energy of shooting stars, and is best worked during one of the annual meteor showers. Bay leaf is a widely popular ingredient in wish magic. To strengthen the spell, try working for a goal related to one of the magical suggestions in the meteor shower descriptions above.

Depending on your practice and personal beliefs, you may want to address this spell to a specific deity or group of deities, or you may simply call on the divine energies of the Universe—use the language that rings most true for you.

You will need:

- A green candle
- Star anise or sandalwood essential oil
- A bay leaf
- A permanent marker

- A fire safe container (such as a small cast iron cauldron)

Directions:

Begin by dressing the candle with a few drops of the essential oil. Light the candle and take a moment to connect with the flame. Close your eyes. With your mind's eye, envision a clear night sky with a bright meteor shower taking place above you.

Watch the shooting stars with awe, knowing they are connecting you to divinity. Take this moment to reflect on your wish. Once you have your wish clear in your mind, open your eyes. Consider two or three words that summarize your wish and write them on the bay leaf with your marker.

Hold the bay leaf in your hand and say the following incantation:

"Divine shooting stars, heavenly gods, hear my wish and make it true!"

Describe your wish as you take the bay leaf and carefully put it over the candle flame. Once it ignites, drop it into the fire safe container. It will burn up very quickly, so be careful!

CONCLUSION: THE AGE OF AQUARIUS

Hopefully, this book has provided you with a basic grounding in astrology and its vast potential for use in magic.

Of course, there is always more to learn—as noted in the Introduction, astrology is a lifetime study (as is magic)! Those interested in further understanding the divine language of the cosmos will find a list of recommended resources at the end of the book. For now, we leave you with this important note about a very special development in our astrological times: the Age of Aquarius.

An astrological age is a time period based on the movement of the Earth in relation to the zodiac. The astrological year begins at the spring equinox, which is the start of Aries season. However, the Earth's wobble causes gradual shifts in the position of the constellations from Earth's perspective, which means that the spring equinox point of the zodiac no longer aligns with the constellation Aries.

In fact, the position of the equinox shifts "backwards," or in a counter-clockwise motion, moving gradually through each sign roughly every 2,160 years. Each period within a sign is known as an astrological age, and marks shifts in humanity's collective experience in terms of history, culture, societal structures, and technological development.

This shifting of the ages is not an exact moment in time, but an estimated or theorized time. Depending on who you ask, the Age of Aquarius began with the Industrial Revolution, or at the birth of the Nuclear Age in the mid-20th century, or at the 2012 Winter Solstice, or at the Vernal Equinox in 2021, or that it will begin at a date in our not-too-distant future. Many believe that if we are not in the Age of Aquarius yet, we are certainly experiencing the transitional energies that come with this new era.

The Age of Aquarius marks the shift out of the Age of Pisces, which saw the dawn of Christianity, but was also an age of spiritual repression in many ways. The Age of Aquarius is said to be a humanitarian time, of expanding consciousness, enlightenment, and an emphasis on community.

We move away from established traditions to find new ways of living that are innovative, artistic, and progressive. Electronics will advance, and the information will travel even more quickly. We are going to further explore space, and some suggest we will have contact with aliens (while others assert that we already have had contact).

On the darker side, there are many who speculate that Aquarian technology may be too advanced for humans, citing 5G networks and AI as examples of things we use, but don't fully grasp the potential dangers of. Because of

Aquarius' radical nature, there are divisions in politics, and misinformation can further cause rifts between people.

Either way we look at it, many people feel like this is a turning point in our history with this planet. As witches, we are fortunate enough to feel those shifts on an intuitive level. We can work with the stars and the elements to align with divinity. This allows us to be supportive healers and mystical magicians who can promote beneficial transitions for ourselves, our loved ones, all of humanity, and the natural world.

Let us hope that the Age of Aquarius initiates a time where the magic and metaphysical properties of the universe are accepted, understood, and utilized to create a balanced and peaceful existence here on Earth.

SUGGESTIONS FOR FURTHER READING

Magical Astrology: Use the Power of the Planets to Create an Enchanted Life. Skye Alexander, 2019.

Astrology for Yourself: A Workbook for Personal Transformation. Douglas Bloch and Demetra George, 2006.

The Complete Book of Incense, Oils, and Brews. Scott Cunningham, 1997.

Astrological Magick. Estelle Daniels, 1995.

Practical Astrology for Witches and Pagans: Using the Planets and the Stars for Effective Spellwork, Rituals, and Magical Work. Ivo Dominguez Jr., 2016.

The Complete Guide to Astrology: Understanding Yourself, Your Signs, and Your Birth Chart. Louise Edington, 2020.

Judy Hall's Crystal Zodiac: Use Birthstones to Enhance Your Life. Judy Hall, 2017.

Astrology for Witches: Enhance Your Rituals, Spells, and Practices with the Magic of the Cosmos. Michael Herkes, 2022.

Tarot and Astrology: Enhance Your Readings with the Wisdom of the Zodiac. Corrine Kenner, 2011.

Llewellyn's Complete Book of Correspondences: A Comprehensive and Cross-Referenced Resource for Pagans and Wiccans. Sandra Kynes, 2013.

The Only Way to Learn Astrology, Volume 1: Basic Principles, 2ⁿᵈ Ed. Marion D March and Joan McEvers, 2008.

You Were Born for This: Astrology for Radical Self-Acceptance. Chani Nicholas, 2020.

Moon Magic. Rachel Patterson, 2014.

Cosmic Health: Unlock Yor Healing Magic with Astrology, Positive Psychology, and Integrative Wellness. Jennifer Racioppi, 2021.

Llewellyn's Complete Book of Astrology: The Easy Way to Learn Astrology. Kris Brandt Riske, 2007.

The Witch's Complete Guide to Astrology: Harness the Heavens and Unlock Your Potential for a Magical Year. Elsie Wild, 2022.

The Only Astrology Book You'll Ever Need: Twenty-First Century Edition. Joanna Martine Woolfolk, 2006.

Weird Astrology. Maighdlin Kelly.

ABOUT THE AUTHORS

Kiki Dombrowski is an active member of the magical community as a teacher, writer, and divination reader. Kiki has a successful writing career, being a long-time writer for *Witch Way Magazine*, a featured writer in Lisa Chamberlain's annual datebook journals, and a co-author for *Witch Way's Book of 100 Love Spells*. Her book *A Curious Future* is a well-loved, critically acclaimed collection of unique and unusual divination techniques. Her newest book, *Transformative Tarot*, is about approaching tarot for self-development and spiritual exploration. Kiki has a BA in English and Creative Writing from Southern Connecticut University and a MA in Medieval Literature from Nottingham University. She has appeared as a guest on numerous popular podcasts, including the Witch Daily Show, Penny Royal Podcast, Conspirinormal, Pagan's Witchy Corner, and 6 Degrees of John Keel. For more information please visit **www.kikidombrowski.com**.

Lisa Chamberlain is the successful author of more than twenty books on Wicca, divination, and magical living, including *Green Witchcraft for Beginners*, *Wicca Book of Herbal Spells*, *Elemental Magic*, *Magic and the Law of Attraction*, *Runes for Beginners,* and *Tarot for Beginners.* An intuitive empath, she has been exploring witchcraft, magic, and other esoteric paths since her teenage years. Her spiritual journey has included a traditional solitary Wiccan practice as well as more eclectic studies across a wide range of belief systems. Lisa's focus is on positive magic that promotes self-empowerment for the good of the whole. You can find out more about her and her work at her website, **www.wiccaliving.com**.

THREE FREE AUDIOBOOKS PROMOTION

Don't forget, you can now enjoy **three audiobooks completely free of charge** when you start a free 30-day trial with Audible.

If you're new to the Craft, *Wicca Starter Kit* contains three of Lisa's most popular books for beginning Wiccans. You can download it for free at:

www.wiccaliving.com/free-wiccan-audiobooks

Or, if you're wanting to expand your magical skills, check out *Spellbook Starter Kit,* with three collections of spellwork featuring the powerful energies of candles, colors, crystals, mineral stones, and magical herbs. Download over 150 spells for free at:

www.wiccaliving.com/free-spell-audiobooks

Members receive free audiobooks every month, as well as exclusive discounts. And, if you don't want to continue with Audible, just remember to cancel your membership. You won't be charged a cent, and you'll get to keep your books!

Happy listening!

MORE BOOKS BY LISA CHAMBERLAIN

Wicca for Beginners: A Guide to Wiccan Beliefs, Rituals, Magic, and Witchcraft

Wicca Book of Spells: A Book of Shadows for Wiccans, Witches, and Other Practitioners of Magic

Wicca Herbal Magic: A Beginner's Guide to Practicing Wiccan Herbal Magic, with Simple Herb Spells

Wicca Book of Herbal Spells: A Book of Shadows for Wiccans, Witches, and Other Practitioners of Herbal Magic

Wicca Candle Magic: A Beginner's Guide to Practicing Wiccan Candle Magic, with Simple Candle Spells

Wicca Book of Candle Spells: A Book of Shadows for Wiccans, Witches, and Other Practitioners of Candle Magic

Wicca Crystal Magic: A Beginner's Guide to Practicing Wiccan Crystal Magic, with Simple Crystal Spells

Wicca Book of Crystal Spells: A Book of Shadows for Wiccans, Witches, and Other Practitioners of Crystal Magic

Tarot for Beginners: A Guide to Psychic Tarot Reading, Real Tarot Card Meanings, and Simple Tarot Spreads

Runes for Beginners: A Guide to Reading Runes in Divination, Rune Magic, and the Meaning of the Elder Futhark Runes

Wicca Moon Magic: A Wiccan's Guide and Grimoire for Working Magic with Lunar Energies

Wicca Wheel of the Year Magic: A Beginner's Guide to the Sabbats, with History, Symbolism, Celebration Ideas, and Dedicated Sabbat Spells

Wicca Kitchen Witchery: A Beginner's Guide to Magical Cooking, with Simple Spells and Recipes

Wicca Essential Oils Magic: A Beginner's Guide to Working with Magical Oils, with Simple Recipes and Spells

Wicca Elemental Magic: A Guide to the Elements, Witchcraft, and Magical Spells

Wicca Magical Deities: A Guide to the Wiccan God and Goddess, and Choosing a Deity to Work Magic With

Wicca Living a Magical Life: A Guide to Initiation and Navigating Your Journey in the Craft

Magic and the Law of Attraction: A Witch's Guide to the Magic of Intention, Raising Your Frequency, and Building Your Reality

Wicca Altar and Tools: A Beginner's Guide to Wiccan Altars, Tools for Spellwork, and Casting the Circle

Wicca Finding Your Path: A Beginner's Guide to Wiccan Traditions, Solitary Practitioners, Eclectic Witches, Covens, and Circles

Wicca Book of Shadows: A Beginner's Guide to Keeping Your Own Book of Shadows and the History of Grimoires

Modern Witchcraft and Magic for Beginners: A Guide to Traditional and Contemporary Paths, with Magical Techniques for the Beginner Witch

FREE GIFT REMINDER

Just a reminder that Lisa is giving away an exclusive, free spell book as a thank-you gift to new readers!

Little Book of Spells contains ten spells that are ideal for newcomers to the practice of magic, but are also suitable for any level of experience.

Read it on read on your laptop, phone, tablet, Kindle or Nook device by visiting:

www.wiccaliving.com/bonus

DID YOU ENJOY *MAGICAL ASTROLOGY FOR WITCHES*?

Thanks so much for reading this book! I know there are many great books out there about Wicca, so I really appreciate you choosing this one.

If you enjoyed the book, I have a small favor to ask—would you take a couple of minutes to leave a review for this book on Amazon?

Your feedback will help me to make improvements to this book, and to create even better ones in the future. It will also help me develop new ideas for books on other topics that might be of interest to you. Thanks in advance for your help!